THE JOURNEY
of a NURSE

*To Michon, &
Christina,
May God be
with you on your
journey.
P. Lenelenge*

THE JOURNEY
of a NURSE

From dreams to degrees

Paulette E. Terrelonge DNP

MILL CITY PRESS

Mill City Press, Inc.
2301 Lucien Way #415
Maitland, FL 32751
407·339·4217
www.millcitypress.net

Printed in the United States of America

ISBN-13: 978-1-54562-264-3

Dedication

This book is dedicated to my children who supported me in my quest for continued education and higher learning and who were my towers of strength as I navigated different aspects of my journey.

Table of Contents

Acknowledgments

I would like to acknowledge the nurse who gave me the address for the University Hospital of the West Indies School of Nursing, all the nurses who mentored and guided me in nursing schools, all the nurses who I worked with, my batch mates, my nursing instructors and committee members. I would also like to acknowledge the pastor and chaplain who inspired me to write this book.

Introduction

Everyone was created for a purpose, and I believe that we were placed in the world to fulfill our God-given destiny. It is our responsibility to pursue ways in which we can achieve the work that God intends for us to do. As human beings and people who can make this world a better place, we must strive to make our contributions for the betterment of mankind. People may take different pathways as they travel along life's journey but they can reach their destinations if they focus on their goals.

I am reminded of the scripture that says, "And He gave some, apostles; and some, prophets; and some, evangelists; and some, pastors and teachers" Ephesians 4:11. I have added: "and He gave some, nurses." It is said that people have different callings in life. I am positive that my calling was to be a nurse.

This is the story of my determination to become a nurse and how I overcame many obstacles to pursue a career in nursing. The goal of sharing my adventurous journey is to encourage others to follow their dreams and to aim for the stars. At my first nursing graduation, the graduates sang, "Climb every mountain, reach for the stars, follow every rainbow, till you find your dream." My dream has been partially fulfilled, so I will continue to climb.

Chapter 1
The Call

My journey to become a nurse started in Jamaica where I was born. I was in the third grade at Christiana Moravian Primary School in the parish of Manchester when my teacher asked the class to write essays about what we would like to be when we grew up. I did not hesitate but began writing my essay that would set the pace for my educational journey. I wrote that I wanted to be a nurse because I wanted to help people. God directed me to pursue science subjects in secondary and high schools although I did not realize that a good knowledge of the sciences was necessary for a career in nursing. I graduated from high school with the determination of pursuing a nursing career.

I applied to Percy Junor Hospital in Spalding, Clarendon where I was born, to do a practical nursing program. I did not know at that time that there were different kinds of nurses. I sat the entrance examination and scored a very high grade. The director of the nursing program at Percy Junor Hospital informed me that I had the qualifications to become a registered nurse, so she gave me the address for the University Hospital of the West Indies School of Nursing. I applied to the University Hospital of the West Indies School of Nursing to be trained as a registered nurse within a few days and patiently waited for the reply.

I anxiously opened the letter I received from the school, but the reply was not what I expected. Receipt of my application was acknowledged, and I was told that I needed a better grade in English and another O-level subject. The requirement was five O-level subjects including English and Mathematics. O-levels were subject-based examinations that were done at the completion of high school.

I enrolled at Knox Community College in Spalding, Clarendon, where a program of study was customized for me. The one year that I spent at Knox Community College was rewarding because I was successful in the three O-level subjects that I did. My customized program was very interesting, and I was the only student doing that program. I attended classes with high school students in grades eleven and twelve as I prepared for the O-level subjects which were English, geography, and history. Some days I had classes with both grade eleven and grade twelve students, so I did the two-year coursework in one year. I repeated English, but history and geography were done at O-level for the first time. Accounting and office management were done with the community college students. It was necessary for me to attend the high school and the community college simultaneously so that I could matriculate as a full-time student.

After leaving Knox Community College I reapplied to the School of Nursing and while waiting on the reply, I got a job at the revenue office in Christiana, Manchester. I was working at the revenue office for about six months when I received another letter from the School of Nursing. I was very excited after reading the letter because, having met all the requirements, I was invited to attend an interview at the school in Kingston, Jamaica. My excitement was mixed with anxiety and apprehension because I had never gone to Kingston, the capital of Jamaica, by myself. I mustered up all the courage I needed and decided to travel to Kingston because my career depended on my going to the interview.

I slept at a friend's home overnight, so it would be easier for me to get transportation to Kingston. My friend lived very close to the town of Christiana and she ensured that I left her home on time to get to Kingston. I left my friend's home early the morning of the interview and after about three hours of travelling by three different buses, I arrived at the school.

I was relieved to be at the University Hospital, and as I entered through the large gates, I breathed a sigh of relief, as if to say, "Yes! I am finally here." When I was a child, people referred to the University Hospital as "UC." It was a great achievement and a thrilling experience for me to be at UC. I followed the directions given to me by the security guard at the gate and soon I was at the School of Nursing, which was across from the University Hospital. I was further directed to the venue for the interview, which was in a room in the nurses' home.

I answered all the questions with ease and I felt very relieved when one of the interviewers said that I would get a letter from the School of Nursing. I left the interview with confidence that I had been accepted into the nursing program. The journey back to my home took a very adventurous path. The big arch with the words "Hope Zoo and Botanical Gardens" caused me to make a quick decision to visit the zoo and botanical gardens.

I stopped the minivan that I was travelling in and darted across the busy highway. I thanked the Lord that I was not hit by an oncoming car and was happy to safely enter through the big gate under the arch.

The zoo and botanical gardens were in close proximity to the nursing school. Many people from all over Jamaica visited the zoo, the botanical gardens, and the amusement park, which were in the same location. These places were also popular places for excursions. Our annual church trip took us many times to the Hope Zoo and Botanical Gardens and to the amusement park. It was during one of these excursions that I learned that the zoo and botanical gardens occupied hundreds of acres of land situated on the Liquanea Plain in the parish of St. Andrew. St. Andrew is an adjoining parish to Kingston. The beautiful pink flamingos and multi-colored peacocks that I saw shortly after entering the zoo aroused my excitement and seemed to propel me further into the zoo.

I overstayed my time in the zoo and botanical gardens. It was years since I last visited those places, so I had to see most of the animals that were in the zoo and experience many of the rides that were in the amusement park, which was adjacent to the zoo. The roller coaster and the tilt-a-whirl were my favorite rides. Holding my abdomen which ached from laugher, I quickly rejoined the lines to experience more fun on those rides. The botanical gardens had some of the most beautiful flowers that I ever saw. I concluded later that I should not have made that detour knowing that I had a three-hour journey to my home and I had to take public transportation.

I left the Hope Zoo and Botanical Gardens and wondered how I was going to get home. Transportation problems started from the onset of the journey. All the minivans were packed with people from the beginning of their routes so that by the time they got to where I was, there was no available room. I waited for a long time and finally a minivan came to my rescue. I was very happy to be on my way home but, realizing that my commute home would be very challenging, I felt sorry for myself. I couldn't get a minivan that was going to Mandeville, where I would get connecting transportation to Christiana, my hometown. I also needed to take a taxi from Christiana to my home. I happily took a minivan that was going to May Pen, which is a town in Clarendon, an adjoining parish to Manchester. A Good Samaritan gave me a ride from May Pen to Mandeville, but I got there after nightfall and that made it harder to get trans-portation to Christiana. After waiting at the usual place for a long time without seeing any vans, I walked to another part of Mandeville town to increase my chances of getting a ride. As the hours passed, I resigned myself to the gruesome reality that I was not going to get any form of transportation at that hour of the night.

I knew someone who lived nearby, but I could not remember which of the houses on the busy street I'd been to only once before. As the people on the road got sparse, I realized that I was in a predicament. A group of people approached me and I was questioned as to why I was on the road at that hour. One of the persons, a total stranger, must have been sorry for me, and I was offered lodging for the night. I was happy to be off the street but was worried about my mother who I knew would be very concerned. There was no way to contact her, as telephones were not available in most homes. I thanked the Good Samaritan for coming to my rescue, but I could not sleep.

I left the home of the stranger early the next morning and took the first minivan to Christiana. Thankful to be in Christiana, I walked to another area of the town to get a taxi to go to my home. After waiting a long time, I got a taxi driven by a driver who was finally satisfied that he got his quota of passengers. I was very relieved when the last seat was taken by a lady with a baby because it increased my chance of getting home and returning to the same town to work. I wanted to be at work on time so that I wouldn't have to explain the reason for my lateness to my boss and other coworkers. I was very disappointed when I got home because my mother was already gone to work so I did not get to tell her about my ordeal. I called her from my workplace and she was very happy to hear that I was safe. I knew that angels watched over me because, on two occasions, I was with complete strangers. I vowed that I would not make such adventurous detours again.

Another letter from the School of Nursing confirmed my acceptance to start training as a staff nurse (registered nurse) in August 1978. A second appearance at the School of Nursing was required before the program officially started. I had to bring in a physical examination form and a dental report. I went to a medical doctor in Christiana, but I had to go to Mandeville, the capital of Manchester, to see a dentist. After an examination of my teeth, the dentist told me that I had some cavities that needed to be filled. I told the dentist that I would fill the cavities at a later date, but I needed the dental report to be filled out. The dentist replied that he could not tell a person with a heart problem that he was healthy, so I had to fill my cavities before he could give me a dental report.

I had travelled about eighteen miles to Mandeville to get to the dentist so I agreed that he should fix my cavities. I left the dental office with a sense of accomplishment because I never had my teeth filled before. The School of Nursing also sent me a book and supplies list. Since the items on the list were not available in my town, I bought some of the books and a bandage scissors in Mandeville. I journeyed home to Christiana with great excitement and was eager to cross things off my list as they were accomplished.

I had another hurdle to cross: getting to the school by 8 a.m., which was a requirement for final acceptance into the nursing program. After praying about the situation, I remembered an old classmate that I'd met in Christiana Secondary School and who had moved to Kingston, the same city as the School of Nursing. I wrote to my friend because a telephone was not readily available, and, after consulting with her parents, she agreed that I could stay at her home the night prior to the meeting at the school. She gave me directions to her home in a letter, and so I boarded a bus in Christiana and had to take a second bus in Mandeville. After about three hours of travelling, I was in Kingston. I arrived at my friend's home with ease because she lived in the first town that was the entry point into Kingston for travelers from the west. My friend also lived near to the bus stop.

My friend and I were happy to see each other again. She was one of my best friends in secondary school, but she and her family had moved to Kingston during the summer before high school. I was very thankful that I kept in touch with her by postal mail for almost five years because she was the only person I remembered who could house me so that I could get to the School of Nursing by 8 a.m. on the morning of the final meeting before the nursing program officially started. After several hours of reminiscing, we went to bed. The next morning, I got out of bed early and got ready for a very exciting day.

Fifty-two prospective nurses met in a classroom at the nursing school. I felt elated and sat in the front of the classroom and paid attention to every word that was uttered by the presenters for the day. We were introduced to the nursing instructors and to each other. It was exciting to hear that we would not have to wait for one or two years to go on the wards but that we would be assigned to wards and allowed to perform patient care after three months. After being told about the nursing program, which had a duration of three years, we were taken to the linen room and given enough pink-striped material (or candy stripes, as the material that made our student nurse's uniforms was also called) to make six uniforms. After the day's activities, one of my batch mates and I went to a bookstore in Kingston where I obtained some additional books. I returned to my friend's home, collected my belongings, and boarded the first of two buses back to Christiana.

Chapter 2
The Official Start

I t was one Sunday in late August 1978, when I left my hometown in Christiana. My mother and the three high school students who were boarding at our home accompanied me to Kingston. Although I was leaving my friends and my church, I was happy to go because I was going to start my career in nursing. I was also excited about leaving the country to live in the nurse's home in Kingston. It was like a dream come true for me to live in the capital of Jamaica. It was my desire to live in Kingston after high school, but my job applications went unanswered.

We arrived at the University Hospital and stopped under the shade of a three-story building to eat the delicious lunch that my mother had prepared. After having lunch, we proceeded to the nurses' home. I was given my room assignment, and my mother assisted me in carrying my belongings to the room. I said goodbye to my mother and the others, and as the van drove out of sight, I felt tears running down my cheeks. This was the first time I had left home for a prolonged period.

Alone in my room, I rehearsed the activities that preceded my being in a strange room and in a home where I would reside for three years. The room had two single beds with a small table between them and two big closets. I stared at the cars as they passed on the road outside my window. It was exciting to see so many vehicles travelling in both directions on the road. I could also see the main gate of the University Hospital and was amazed to see the great numbers of people and motor vehicles entering and leaving the hospital. I unpacked my clothes and then sat on one of the beds and stared at the wall. The quietness of the room was interrupted by some noise in the hallway outside of my room.

I looked in the hallway and recognized a familiar face. It was a batch mate I had met the day we had to report to the school two weeks before. There was more talking as other students arrived. One of the students asked me if I went to the cafeteria. I told her that I did not, and she offered to go with me. She had come in earlier and had found the cafeteria. I was not hungry, but I had to go to the cafeteria at that time or I would not get supper. The trip to the cafeteria was an adventurous one. We walked across a parking lot then through the hospital, made several turns, and walked long corridors. The cafeteria was located inside of the hospital and was also used by the hospital staff. It was the largest cafeteria that I had ever seen. There were nurses in their white uniforms, student nurses in their pink-striped uniforms, people in lab coats, and many others. We had a delicious supper then we went back to our rooms to prepare for the next day. My roommate arrived that night and after talking for a long time we went to bed. I lay awake in the quietness of the night and reflected upon the events of the day.

Fifty-two excited student nurses assembled in a classroom at the University Hospital of the West Indies School of Nursing. On a Monday morning in late August 1978, batch 82 was formed. The batch was comprised of student nurses from all over Jamaica, two from Grenada, two from Antigua, and one from the Virgin Islands. During the first break of the day, one of the nursing instructors asked me to call Nurse Chin. I asked her who Nurse Chin was and soon realized that she was referring to one of my batch mates. We were already called nurses, and I immediately reflected that my childhood dream of becoming a nurse was becoming a reality.

The first day as a student nurse was well spent. My batch mates and I were thrilled to learn about the School of Nursing, meet the different nursing instructors, and learn about our program of study for the next three years. We were informed that our rooms were all located in the same section of the nurses' home called PTS Block. Two of my batch mates and I shared the same first name, so my other batch mates had an added task of specifying which of the three Paulettes they were referring to. After a full day of orientation, followed by supper in the cafe-teria, my batch mates and I retired to our rooms.

I was awakened early the following morning by shouts. I looked through my window and saw a group of people singing and shouting. They were saying different things about Bastille. My batch mates and I gathered in the hallways of the nurses' home and were very puzzled, as we did not know what the singing and shouting were for. We were later informed that the people who were singing and shouting were students from the University of the West Indies and that, that was their way of wel-coming us to the School of Nursing and to the university campus which we shared. I later discovered that Bastille was a French prison. I did not see the connection because the nurses' home was far from being like a prison. I can only remember one restriction and it was that male visitors were not allowed in our rooms. We could leave the nurses' home without getting permission and there was no curfew. I also thought that the nurses' home was one of the safest places to live in Kingston.

During the first weeks, we visited the Mona Water Treatment Plant and other interesting places that were in close proximity to the School of Nursing. This was very exciting to me because I came from a rural area in Jamaica and had never visited those places. When I was in secondary school, I learned about plains (large areas of flat land) in social studies and to be living and studying on the Liguanea Plain gave me the reassurance that the quest for education would take me to places that I otherwise would not have gone. I also discovered that the College of Arts, Science and Technology—now University of Technology—and the United Theological College of the West Indies were in close proximity to the School of Nursing.

Living across from the University Hospital of the West Indies was filled with excitement. The sounds of helicopters made my batch mates and I abandoned whatever we were doing and run to the closest point in the nurses' home where we could safely see what was going on. University Hospital was one of the largest hospitals in Jamaica and patients from all over Jamaica and other islands in the West Indies were taken to the University Hospital for medical care. Helicopters were frequently used to transport very sick patients.

My batch mates and I spent about three months in the classroom pursuing subjects such as fundamentals of nursing, chemistry for nurses, and psychology. Our first official visit to the hospital wards was very exciting. We were dressed in our pink candy-striped uniforms and white caps with flutes that we had to make by using needle and thread. We also wore white aprons and white shoes. We had white pins with our names inscribed in pink, and, since my pin was P. Ashley (my maiden name), I was called Pashley by my batch mates, so the task of identifying the three Paulettes was reduced.

Chapter 3
The Wards

Most of our time was spent on the wards in the hospital. Every six weeks my batch mates and I were rotated to different wards. My first ward assignment was a surgical floor. My duties included bed baths, bed making, making drinks and serving fluids to the patients, serving meals, doing intake and output sheets, accompany patients to the operating room, and writing progress notes. Some days I was assigned to the sluice room. The sluice room had racks with bedpans, urinals, vomit bowls, a flush for the dirty bedpans and a sterilizer. Bedpans, urinals, and vomit bowls were made from aluminum and had to be washed and sterilized after use. I also had to wash and roll bandages. The shifts initially were 7 a.m. to 3 p.m. and then I was assigned noon to 8 p.m. In a week, I did various combinations of 7 a.m. to 3 p.m. and noon to 8 p.m. I also worked one to two weekends per month, and I was given two days off per week.

Taking care of patients was very satisfying for me. I looked forward to going on the wards each day. I executed my daily tasks with pleasure and most of the patients showed appreciation and gratitude for any help rendered to them. One of my first patients was a man who had an amputation of one of his legs. There were times when he said that he had pain in the leg that was amputated. I wished that I could help him but I could not and I did not understand how it was possible to have pain in a limb that was not there. Another patient I was honored to meet was a very popular comedian in Jamaica. I listened to him on the radio when I was a child, so I was elated to meet him. The first six weeks passed very quickly, and then it was time to go to another ward.

I woke early the morning that I had to report to my new ward. After having breakfast in the cafeteria, I reported for duty on the medical ward. I had heard from some of my batch mates who were previously assigned to this ward that the patients were very sick and that the work was hard. The routine on this ward was different from that on the ward that I worked before. I did not mix drinks on this ward, but I fed more patients and did pressure area care. Most of the patients were bedridden and required total care.

I anxiously awaited my subsequent rotations and was very eager to get new experiences on the other wards. We had blocks of classes in the Nursing School so my batch mates and I were prepared before we were sent to different wards. On the orthopedic ward, I was impressed with the Stryker frame beds for patients with spinal injuries. The Stryker frame beds were used to turn patients from their abdomens to their backs and vice versa. Sometimes if I could not get help to turn my patients on the Stryker frame beds, I turned them alone. The patients were very thankful, and I was happy that I could help to make them more comfortable. I was fascinated to see patients with fractures of the femur on tractions with different weights. My tasks of making beds for those patients were made easier as the patients would lift themselves off the bed by holding on to the bars or strings over their beds.

The children's wards were located beside each other and in another building in very close proximity to the main hospital building. I enjoyed feeding and changing the babies, as this was the first time I had taken care of babies. I also accompanied babies to the X-ray department and worked in the formula room. There were no ready-to-feed formulas. Formulas were mixed ahead of time. They were then bottled and labeled with the names of all the babies on the three different children's wards. The bottled formulas were kept in refrigerators on the wards and heated in large pots prior to feeding the babies. I also assisted in holding the babies for different procedures such as lumbar puncture and the insertion of intravenous lines and collected urine and stool samples for testing. I always completed my assignments because I loved what I did.

The experience I gained on the gynecology ward was exciting and broadened my knowledge of the human body. Patients on that floor had varied gynecological problems. The evenings before gynecological surgeries were very busy. I was involved in preparing the patients for surgery by giving enemas, douches, and shaving the patients. On the day of surgery, I accompanied the patients to the operating room. I remembered working on the gynecology ward one night when it rained so hard that most of the staff nurses who lived off the hospital's campus could not come to work. Three student nurses and I worked on the ward, and I was very thankful for the experience because I worked independently without a staff nurse.

The emergency room was a very busy area to work. I saw illnesses that I was seeing for the first time. The first day that I was assigned to the emergency room I was scared when I saw a man having an asthma attack. He could hardly breathe, and it appeared as if he was going to die. My anxiety was allayed by a staff nurse who informed me that many patients with asthma came to the emergency room and they did not die. Asthmatics were treated initially in the treatment room of the emergency room in three cubicles with stretchers, which were holding areas for asthmatics who needed medications intravenously. I took care of those patients, making sure that they had their medications on time and that their other needs were met.

The minor operating theater was another exciting place to work. Procedures such as suturing of lacerations, dilatation and curettage, and endoscopies were done there. I assisted in these procedures, then washed and prepared the instruments for sterilization. I also helped to prepare the rooms for the different procedures.

My experience in labor and delivery was the deciding factor for my nursing career. I decided that after graduation from general training I would become a midwife. I observed deliveries and cesarean sections and I assisted in bathing the patients after deliveries, set delivery tables, weighed and fed babies. I also helped with transporting mothers and their babies to the postpartum wards. The next rotation took me to the postpartum unit.

The care I rendered to the postpartum mothers was beyond my imagination. The salt soaks and heat treatment that I gave to women who had episiotomies or vaginal lacerations during birth were new experiences I had no knowledge of before. I also took care of women who had cesarean sections. The first two days after surgery appeared to be the hardest for most of these women who required pain medication every four hours. I assisted them with their care as well as taking care of their babies. This was very fulfilling and meant a great deal to me as this was the first time that I was taking care of new-born babies.

The experience I had on the psychiatric ward was very exciting. There were many patients with varying mental conditions. I observed patients having electro-shock therapy, and I assisted in preparing them for the procedure and monitored them afterward. The day room was an exciting place to work. The staff planned concerts for the patients in which the patients were the main performers. The display of talents was amazing and was also entertaining to the staff who worked on the unit.

I had heard that nurses worked at nights when I was a child, and I wondered what it would be like to work at nights. The time had come for me to experience night duty. I was still a student nurse when I was placed on night duty. I was assigned to different wards with one staff nurse most nights, so when the staff nurse was on her lunch break, I was alone on the wards with the patients. Night shift also made me feel like a nurse since nursing is one of the professions where working at nights is a necessity. I enjoyed my nights off. I had more time to do other things because I only worked thirteen twelve-hour shifts in a month. The cafeteria was open at nights and we were served cooked meals. In the mornings after work, I had breakfast in the cafeteria and then walked tiredly to the nurses' home. My bed was very enticing, and, after having a shower, I closed my windows to make the room as dark as possible, then went to sleep. The windows were not made with glass but some other material that successfully kept the daylight out of my room.

I was very hungry when I awoke, but I could not go to the cafeteria because I had one meal ticket and I needed to get lunch at nights when I worked. I asked the kind nurse who supervised us in the nurses' home for a second meal ticket and she gave it to me. Every morning before I went to bed I placed my covered container labeled with my name and my second meal ticket in a designated place for containers. In the afternoon when I woke up, I went downstairs for my lunch, which a worker collected from the cafeteria in the hospital. I was very thankful that I did not get overweight from eating two lunches plus breakfast and dinner three days per week for about six weeks.

Chapter 4
Extracurricular Activities

N urses Week was welcomed every year, and activities such as the crowning of Miss University Hospital and the selection of the student nurse of the year were very exciting. There were other activities throughout the year that I participated in. One of them was Christian Fellowship. Christian Fellowship consisted of student nurses from all the batches and staff nurses who lived in the nurses' home. There were about five or six batches of student nurses in the school of nursing at one time. We met once per week in a room with a piano and some-times we had guests from neighboring institutions. We went to camps, had prayer walks, and had evangelistic meetings at the nurses' home. We also visited Christian fellowships at College of Arts, Science and Technology (CAST) and the University of the West Indies.

Christian Fellowships from all over Kingston participated in a rally that was held in Shooters Hill, Manchester. The ride was long but we had a good time singing and admiring the countryside as the train moved along very swiftly and without interruption. We got off the train at Kendal, Manchester, and walked about half a mile to a sports club where the rally convened. I was especially happy to go on this trip because it was not far from my mother's home. I left the rally and made a quick visit to my mother's home, having planned my departure very well. I did not want to miss singing with the nurses' chorale, so I went after we sang. I departed on a twelve-mile journey to my mother's home. All along the way I was praying that she would be home as this was a surprise visit. As I entered the home, I opened the gate quietly, but, not wanting to scare her, I called her name loudly. My mother was happy to see me and then became a little sad when I told her that I could only spend a few minutes with her. I ate a piece of the chicken she was frying then left hurriedly to return to the rally before it was over. I also did not want to miss the train going back to Kingston.

The walk to the train station felt longer than when we came the same way that morning. The number of us seemed more than when we went to the rally. Many other people came to the rally who were not from Kingston and so it made the group look so much larger. I went as close as possible to the road bank whenever a motor vehicle was coming. The road was very narrow and I wanted to give the drivers as much of the road as was possible. There were no sidewalks. I still recall how scared I was when a truck ran over one of my friend's feet. We were walking home from school one evening when a truck came around a deep bend. My friend was on the left side of the road and did not get to cross to the other side. Motor vehicles drive on the left side of the road in Jamaica. She went as close as possible to the road bank but there was not enough room for her and the truck. She was out of school for a long time with crushed toes. I did not want to be a victim of the same fate. I was very thankful to arrive at the train station safely. We boarded the train back to Kingston. As the train pulled into the station in Kingston, I realized that many, like me, had fallen asleep. We got to Kingston late and it was not easy to get transportation to the nurses' home. A few taxis came and loaded up very fast. When the last taxi left, we didn't know if or when another one would come. After a few hours, all the student nurses were safely in the nurses' home. The students from the other colleges also got home safely because we did not hear anything to the contrary.

Some of my batch mates and I attended church at the Bethel Baptist Church in Half-Way-Tree, Kingston. Bethel Baptist Church formed a branch that held services in a large lecture room at College of Arts, Science and Technology (CAST). This was very convenient to the nurses as it was within walking distance from the nurses' home. We were happy when a Baptist church was built in Papine, the nearest town to the School of Nursing, so the worshippers at CAST had a church of their own.

I was on my way to church one Sunday morning when a sudden and hard shower of rain came down. I ran as fast as I could, but by the time I got to church, which was not far away, I was soaked. The rain stopped as suddenly as it started and I had no choice but to go back to the nurses' home. It did not rain again for the rest of the day.

Some of my batch mates and I attended Deeper Life Ministries, which was an interdenominational group that met first at the Courtley Manor Hotel in New Kingston and later moved to other hotels in downtown Kingston. Some Saturday evenings we attended Youth for Christ, a religious organization that had excellent programs for young people. One Saturday night, some of my batch mates and I waited at the bus stop for a very long time for a bus to take us downtown Kingston where we would attend Youth for Christ. We did not get the bus we wanted, so we took another bus, which went on a long route. By the time we got to our destination, the Youth for Christ meeting was almost over. We were still happy to meet friends that we had not seen for a long time.

I went to many places with my batch mates. One of the other Paulettes and I went to Jamaica School of Agriculture in St. Catherine to visit her brother, and I met some friends that I went to high school with. I was thrilled to meet some of my high school classmates when I visited the University of the West Indies with another batch mate.

I was a member of Circle K, which was a part of Kiwanis International. Kiwanis International is a service club that assists needy families and hosts activities that benefit the community. The only bingo game I ever attended was sponsored by the Kiwanis club. We had weekly meetings and planned activities that our sponsor, the local Kiwanis club, supported. We went to Kiwanis meetings at the Four Seasons Hotel in Kingston occasionally and had delicious meals at the hotel. Circle K rallies were held in different locations in Jamaica, and the opportunities to get away from Kingston and the nurses' home were always welcomed. Election of new officers for Circle K took place during a convention that lasted for three days at a hotel downtown Kingston. Some members of Circle K, including me, stayed at the hotel. This was another new experience for me, as I had never stayed in a hotel before. It was also the first time that I was in a building so high. My room was many floors above the ground floor, and the view of downtown Kingston from my window was very beautiful. The scenery, which included the Caribbean Sea, was more than I expected to see when I checked into the hotel.

Netball games were held annually and all the batches participated. One year, Batch 82, the batch that I was a member of, was the champion and we ran through the entire nurses' home singing songs of victory. I did not play, but I was at every game cheering the team on. Another fun activity was going to the pool on the university campus. I could not swim, but I enjoyed being in the pool. I watched my batch mates swim and wished that I had the courage to do likewise. Many Jamaicans learned to swim in rivers or the sea. I did not live near a river, and I went to the beach only once per year on trips. I was mostly interested in enjoying the water, and sometimes the lifeguard would allow me to float in the pool using the mechanical floaters. I remembered my "near-drowning" experience and I think that was a factor that prevented me from learning to swim. It was New Year's Day of my first year in high school, and I was excited as usual to be at the beach. It was the annual church "outing" as it was sometimes called. I accepted the offer of a friend to go into the water, and shortly after I was gasping for air. I was covered by the sea and my entire life flashed before me. I cried out to the Master of the sea to save me and He did. I had pain in my right wrist for many days after. I guessed that I was fighting with the water.

The annual pantomime at the Ward Theater was well attended by nursing students. We went in small groups, and I was always inspired by the brilliance of the actors. The theater, which was located downtown Kingston, was beautifully designed and enhanced my enjoyment of the pantomimes. Some of my batch mates and I also attended plays and dance performances at the University of the West Indies.

My batch had concerts and other fundraising activities in the nurses' home. One day as part of our nursing program, we visited the Hillcrest Nursing Home in Kingston. My batch mates and I had a concert for the residents after completing our assigned tasks of bathing them, combing their hair, and feeding them. The residents expressed their gratitude to us and we were happy that they enjoyed the concert because the selections rendered were part of our repertoire for an upcoming concert at the nurses' home. Batch 82 was honored to have a popular radio announcer in Jamaica be the Master of Ceremonies for one of our concerts. That concert was well attended and we were very thankful that it was successful.

Chapter 5
Second Home

The first Sunday afternoon when I entered the nurses' home, I was surprised by the number of steps I had to climb. I have always lived in one-story houses, and the schools that I attended only had one or two floors. My room in the nurses' home was on the third floor and there was no elevator. The room had two single beds made with white sheets and a folded spread was on one of the beds. There was also a table, and two large closets. I selected the closet and the bed away from the door. The tile floor was shiny and was also different because all the houses that I lived in had wooden floors. The bathrooms were across the hall and, as I looked into the bathroom, I was very surprised to see how big it was. There were about six showers, six toilets, and four basins. The laundry room was on another block.

My classmates and I lived on the PTS block for about six months, then we moved to another block. I shared a small room with the same roommate I had on the PTS block, then we were given single rooms that we lived in until we graduated. Male visitors were not allowed on the floors, so when my male cousin visited me, we sat outside on a wooden bench.

I looked forward to my monthly stipend, which was about JA$54 per month. In 1978, that was equivalent to about US$30–35. My first stipend was especially welcome as the little money I brought to Kingston with me was almost finished. Food and housing were deducted, so I could spend the money I received freely. I accepted the offer from one of my batch mates who was going to the bank and offered to change my first stipend check for me. After finishing work at 3 p.m., I rushed to my room and anxiously awaited her return from the bank. I was very disappointed when I was told that she could not change my check.

I took the bus to a bank in Liguanea, and joined a very long line. I was happy to finally be at the head of the line and hurried to the counter when the bank teller called for the next person. I presented what I thought to be the check to the bank teller and was very disappointed when I was told that, that was not the check. I had separated the check from the pay stub and left the check in the nurses' home about two to three miles from the bank. The trips to the nurses' home and back to the bank seemed to be longer than they really were, but finally my check was changed, and I was on my way back to the nurses' home.

Subsequent checks were changed at a bank on the campus of the University of the West Indies, which was within walking distance from the nurses' home. Every payday a representative from the payroll department in the hospital came to the nurses' home to distribute checks. I was very happy to receive my monthly stipend and I was very thankful that I did not have to pay tuition. I might not be a nurse today if I'd had to pay tuition because my mother could not afford to pay it.

When I lived on the PTS block, my bed sheets were changed by the housekeeper once per week, but after that, I had to go to the linen truck that was parked in the nurses' home once per week. I had to wash my sheets several times because I was at work and not able to exchange my dirty sheets for clean ones. My uniforms were also laundered for me by a company that collected the dirty uniforms twice per week. Since I had to be on the wards five days per week, I could not afford to forget to put my laundry bag with my dirty uniforms in the outgoing bin.

I participated in different activities with my batch mates. I attended Christian Fellowship with one group, Circle K with another, and studied with another group. I was fortunate to be accepted by all my batch mates. I also realized that there would never be another Batch 82 at the University of the West Indies School of Nursing. We laughed together, cried together, and got nervous together. Whether we were preparing for local examinations or preparing for the Nursing Council examination — which is like the State Boards in the USA — we were all united and hoped that everyone would be successful.

While living on the PTS block, which was the wing of the nurse's home that housed the newest batch of student nurses, my room was cleaned every day except weekends. One weekend I decided to clean my room. I found the housekeeper's bucket and put some water in it. The bucket, which was on wheels, overturned and water went everywhere. No sooner had I mopped that water and refilled the bucket, than it overturned again. That was the first and last time I used that bucket.

I felt safe living in the nurses' home. When I was living in the country, I heard of crimes happening in Kingston, but in all the years I lived at the nurses' home,

I didn't hear of any crime in the area around the nurses' home. One year the nurses' home was used as a polling station. That year I exercised my franchise and voted for the first and only time in Jamaica.

The three years and two months that I spent in the nurses' home as a student nurse were very enjoyable ones. The atmosphere was very peaceful, which enhanced my learning. The ambiance of the nursing home and the environment was so pleasant that it far exceeded my expectations. I had colds and hoarseness, so I went to the "sick bay" in the nurses' home to be seen by the doctor on more than one occasion. I remembered him telling me to whisper and take Panadol. Panadol was a drug like Tylenol that was widely used for pain and fever in Jamaica. The kind nurse who worked with the doctor and who also supervised the nurses' home, made sure that I had my meals and my medications.

I lived in August Town with my aunt when I was a child. I did not know what part of Jamaica August Town was, but I discovered that it neighbored Mona, where the nurses' home was located. I was delighted when I visited August Town during my Community Health rotation. It was with great anticipation that I went to the Health Clinic at the University of the West Indies to meet the Community Health Aid. As I walked on the road that I must have walked several times as a child, I felt a sense of déjà vu.

Chapter 6
The Nursing Program

M ost of my time was spent on the wards where I had practical experiences that made learning the theory that I was taught in the classroom easier. I was happy to be on the wards, but it was also fun to visit other places that enhanced my nursing experience. I visited the Mona Rehabilitation Center not far from the school. I listened attentively as some of my batch mates and I were informed that some patients who entered the Mona Rehabilitation Center with altered mobility left the center completely rehabilitated and that they returned to their former ways of life. Every aspect of nursing was completely new to me. I had seen only one sick person prior to attending nursing school, so the desire to become a nurse was an inspiration from God.

We also visited other hospitals that had services not offered at the University Hospital or that specialized more in those services. For example, the National Chest Hospital in Liguanea had patients with tuberculosis, and I learned about the treatment for those patients. Bellevue Hospital was the hospital that specialized in mental illness. My batch mates and I spent several weeks at Bellevue Hospital learning and working with patients with mental illness. We also visited the Kingston Public Hospital and observed patients having radiation treatment. These visits were planned simultaneously with the area of nursing we were studying in the classroom so that we could relate better to what we observed and learned in those hospitals.

My batch mates and I had blocks of classes that alternated with time spent on the wards. We were lectured by the nursing instructors and doctors of different specialties who worked at University Hospital. We had to pass each block before we could continue the nursing program. My batch mates and I studied diligently and, with the usage of the nursing and medical libraries, were successful in our examinations. Most evenings after super one of my batch mates and I studied in the medical library until 10 p.m. when the library closed. I also woke up early in the mornings and studied before going on the wards. My Community Health experience was very rewarding and a chance to leave the hospital setting. The family I worked with as a student nurse was physically well but was chosen by my instructor because they needed social services and educational advice. The swinging bridge to Kintyre, St. Andrew, where this family lived was scary to me at first, but I developed the skill of crossing it. Instead of stepping slowly on each piece of board that previously moved under my feet, I held on to the ropes at the sides and ran across the bridge, being careful not to look down at the Hope River below.

Three years came and went, and soon it was time to take the Nursing Council examination. The final two weeks were spent in the classroom reviewing work previously learned. My batch mates and I presented different topics of the curriculum. During that time, we also made plans for our valedictory service. We encountered a major obstacle in our planning. The Mona Chapel on the university campus, which had held the previous valedictory services for the School of Nursing, was not available for our service.

We searched for another church and a church in Half-Way-Tree opened its doors and let us in. Frequent trips to the church for rehearsal were costly, as we had to travel by public transportation. Travelling to the valedictory service in our uniforms on public transportation was also unusual because we were previously taken everywhere by the hospital vans. The valedictory service was a success and we were happy to pass that milestone. One of the songs that the batch rendered at the service was "Climb Ev'ry Mountain," which inspired me to work as hard as possible and reminded me that I could be successful at whatever I do. I also felt that there was nothing out of my reach, so I purposed in my heart to aim high.

I studied earnestly for the Nursing Council examination, which lasted two days. I did not sleep well the night before the examination. The thought of failing the examination, which would hinder me from becoming a staff nurse kept passing through my mind. I remembered the words of one of my batch mates: "What all have, done, one can do." I think that she was implying that all the other nurses that did the Nursing Council examination passed, so each of us would also pass. I was also reassured that I studied everything from the first to the last lecture.

I was nervous going to the examination site on the two days that the examination was convened. I was relieved when I saw the contents of the different papers and realized that I could do all the questions. Examinations in Jamaica were not like it was in the USA. There were no multiple-choice questions. They were all essay questions and each one took about half an hour to complete. On each of the papers, there were about five or six essays to write. I handed in my final paper and was relieved that all my studies to become a staff nurse were over. I do not remember the journey back to the nurses' home, but I knew that I was overjoyed and for the first time I could really relax and did not have anything to study. It was with mixed emotions that I packed all my belongings and prepared to give up my room. I was going to miss my batch mates and the place that had been my home for three years and two months, but I was happy that I was going home to spend time with my mother. In the days that followed, my batch mates said goodbye and one by one we left the nurses' home.

I was hoping that I would be employed at the university hospital after I passed the Nursing Council examination, so I left a bookcase, a fan, a hot plate, and some of my clothes in storage at the nurses' home. I had written to my mother and told her that I was coming home. This time was different from all the other times that I had gone home. I had finished my nursing program and I knew that my mother would be very happy for me.

Chapter 7
Homecoming

I left the nurses' home one day in October 1981 after securely putting away the items I was leaving behind. I took three mini-buses and a taxi, and the three-hour journey gave me some time to reflect on my life as a student nurse and compose myself before meeting my mother. I had visited my home several times since I left for nursing school, but this time it was different. I was going to be home for a longer time while I waited for the results of the Nursing Council examination. As I got closer to my home, I reflected on some of the things that I would do and was hoping that I would get home after my mother came from work.

My mother saw me as I opened the gate and she ran to meet me. She helped me carry my suitcase and bags inside the house. My bags were heavy and the relief I got from carrying them was wonderful. We went into the kitchen where my mother was preparing dinner and we spoke for a long time. Although I wrote letters to my mother from the nurses' home, we did not communicate everything to each other. Telephones were not available in many homes including my mother's. The only time I spoke with her was when I visited her. My mother lived alone because the three high school students who lived with us and accompanied me to Kingston at the start of my nursing career were living with other families. My stepfather died when I was in high school and I did not grow up with my other brothers and sisters.

The days at home were spent doing housework, listening to radio, and reading. Most of the books I read were borrowed from the library. Some of the friends that I had before I went to nursing school were now in colleges or living in other parts of Jamaica, so I did not get to see them. I went to the church that I attended before I went to nursing school and was happy to see some of my old church members. They welcomed me back and I felt like a part of them again.

After about two weeks, I started thinking a lot about the results of the examination. I asked my mother to go to the post office every day because I was expecting the results. One evening my mother brought home the letter that I was expecting. I was so nervous that I could not open the letter. I asked my mother to open it, and after my mother read the first line I started to shout. I had passed the Nursing Council examination and was elated to be a staff nurse. My childhood dream of becoming a nurse was now a reality and I was very thankful to God and to my mother for all her support.

I spent the next few days thinking about my next actions. I had applied for a nursing position at the University Hospital of the West Indies after I sat the Nursing Council examination. One day I was at home alone and I heard someone calling my name. I went to the gate to see my father who was a postman at the post office in Christiana, the town in which we lived. He had brought a telegram, which said that I was to report to University Hospital. I shared this information with my mother when she came from work and we decided that I should go the next day. I spent a part of the night packing my clothes then I went to bed, but I could not sleep. I was overjoyed to think that I was going to work as a staff nurse in one of the most prestigious hospitals in Jamaica.

I reflected on all the time I spent studying and that it finally paid off. I thought of my other batch mates and wondered what plans they were making. I thought about the nurses' home and imagined myself living there again. I used to watch the staff nurses as they entered and left the nurses' home and wondered how much different their rooms were from those of the student nurses. I prayed for the night to pass and I remembered a book that I read titled "Until the Day Breaks and the Shadows Flee." Although this book was not talking about a literal day, it reassured me that the morning would come. And it sure did.

Chapter 8
The New Start

I left home again knowing that it would be more permanent this time. I did not get to say goodbye to my church members because of the suddenness of my departure. My suitcase was heavy, but I had to take public transportation because there was no other way to get to Kingston. I could not afford to charter a minivan as my mother did when I was going to start the nursing program. The long journey to Kingston gave me enough time to plan what I was going to do when I got to Kingston. I could not get to the nurses' home fast enough. I struggled with my suitcase from Papine, the closest town to the nurses' home and the end of the route for most public transportation. I was encouraged, knowing that this would be the last time I would be carrying a heavy suitcase to the nurses' home. I left my suitcase at the nurses' home and hurried to the nursing office at the University Hospital. Some of my batch mates were already in the nursing office and others came later. We completed application forms, had interviews, and were told that orientation would begin in one and a half weeks. I was very disappointed that I did not get a room in the nurses' home because I could not afford to rent an apartment. Eventually I had to take an apartment from which I had to commute by two buses to the hospital. I did not know how I was going to make the initial payment of the rent since I was not working and the little money that was left from my last stipend as a student nurse was almost gone. I borrowed the money from a Kiwanis club member who was a business man and I returned it after I got my first salary.

I made another trip to my mother's home and gave my dressmaker who lived nearby some uniforms to make. I was very happy to get uniform material from a staff nurse who I went to high school with because I had no money to buy white uniforms. I also received a white uniform that was already made from another nurse. I spend another week at my mother's home while waiting for my dressmaker to make my uniforms. The three uniforms were made to my specifications, and I felt happy as I fitted them and imagined myself wearing them on the wards. I went back to Kingston to my new furnished apartment. I could not afford to buy curtains for the windows, so I borrowed some used ones from a nurse who I knew when I was a child in Christiana, Manchester. She and her family had moved to Kingston, and I visited them occasionally while I was in nursing school.

I was given a room in the nurses' home on the H block after one month. I was very happy and I moved from my apartment shortly after. I solicited the help of one of the van drivers from the hospital and was happy to climb the four flights of stairs to my room, which was at the end of the hall. There were no elevators, so I went up and down the stairs several times per day because I went to my room for lunch every day. Each floor had a kitchen and we prepared our own meals. The days of going to the cafeteria for all our meals were over.

Refrigerator space was limited and so one of the first things I bought was a refrigerator. I had to discard the first chicken I bought in the nurses' home. I searched for freezer space on the four floors of the H block, but, not finding any space, I put my chicken on the middle shelf of the refrigerator on the third floor. By the time I was ready to cook the chicken, it was spoilt. My room was small but I managed to fit my refrigerator and my bookcase into it. The original pieces of furniture were a small bed, a chest of drawers, a table, and a closet with shelves. I bought a 17-inch color television next. A color television was a luxury in Jamaica in 1982. Most people who could afford televisions had black and white ones. I was happy to live in the nurses' home again because I thought that the nurses' home was one of the safest places to live in Kingston. Security guards were on duty at every entry point and the nurses' home was well lit. I enjoyed living in the nurses' home for many reasons: I did not have to commute far to work and I saved on bus fare, the amount I paid for rent was much less than what I paid for an apartment, and I could still go to Christian Fellowship regularly.

Living in the nurses' home had some challenges. I had to wash my clothes in the bathroom and take it down four flights of stairs to hang them on the clothesline to dry. I could not wash when I wanted to. I had to check for the availability of line space, which I did from my window. Grocery shopping was once per month. A trip to a supermarket in Liguanea met all my food shopping needs. The kind taxi drivers who took my groceries and I from the supermarket to the nurses' home had to make several trips with the groceries from the taxi to my room on the fourth floor, climbing the stairs. Tipping was not common in Jamaica, so the most the taxi drivers would get after receiving the fare were pleasant "thank-yous."

Looking back, I am thankful for those four flights of stairs that I climbed every day for about two years. I never had to worry about gaining weight when I lived in the nurses' home. I weighed a little over 100 pounds when I became a staff nurse, then I gained a few more pounds after I had my son. I gained the most weight after I migrated to the USA. It seemed that the use of elevators and owning a car contributed to my weight gain.

Chapter 9
On Becoming a Staff Nurse

I t was with a sense of great accomplishment that I dressed in my white uniform one Monday morning in late November 1981. The commute to the hospital could not be faster. This was my first day of orientation. My batch mates and I were very excited and overwhelmed to be staff nurses. Orientation lasted for two weeks and then my first assignment was in the emergency room. I rotated quickly through all the different areas in the emergency room and soon it was time for night duty. I was very thrilled to go on night duty not only because I was glad for the experience of working at night but also because I loved the nights off. I worked on the Sunday or Wednesday schedule. I worked either every Sunday, Monday, Tuesday, and one Saturday every four weeks or every Wednesday, Thursday, Friday, and one Saturday every four weeks.

With so many days off, I decided to get a second job. I had co-workers who were doing "sessions" (working shifts) at Bustamante Hospital for Children and so I went in pursuit of employment at that hospital. I was hired immediately and soon realized that there were many nurses who were working at the Bustamante Children's Hospital but their primary employers were other hospitals. I worked three days every week at Bustamante Children Hospital on all units. This was the only children's hospital in Jamaica, so I saw children with all kinds of illnesses.

Regretfully I was taken off nights at my primary job and rotated through the minor operating theater and observation wards. My next assignment was the out-patient clinics. I worked in all the clinics and I was off every weekend, so I went to church every weekend. I could only work at Bustamante Hospital for Children about once per week, but I was satisfied because I had saved enough money to buy a refrigerator, a television, and a "what-not". A what-not is a piece of furniture that resembles a small wall unit. It had about three shelves, a cupboard with two doors on the lower part of the unit, and four beautifully curved legs. It was brown stained and glistened with the sheen of varnish.

The University Hospital nursing pins that were ordered from London, England, arrived and the news quickly spread through the nurses' home. I hurried to the School of Nursing to purchase one and I wore it with confidence. It is now in the right top drawer of my dressing table. I look at it occasionally and I still get a similar feeling to the one I got on the first day I wore it. It is a small, circular, metallic pin. "University Hospital of the West Indies" is inscribed in the white border, and the middle has a pelican with a red background.

Graduation was held at the University of the West Indies in April 1982 for Batch 82 and Batch 83. I accepted my diploma with satisfaction and was reassured that my hard work had paid off. I was very surprised to get an award for the most helpful student. My mother and some of her friends had journeyed from Christiana the day of graduation and returned home that night. Some of my batch mates and I went to the nurses' home rejoicing that we graduated as staff nurses and for having received our nursing diplomas.

I continued working in the outpatient department for another year and then I was transferred to a medical-surgical ward. This ward had more critically ill patients than the other wards that I worked before. It was a step down from ICU. The experience was new since I did not work on that ward as a student nurse. I was always willing to learn new things and so I accepted the challenge. I was on day shift for about two months then I was put on night duty. Night shift was not welcomed at that time because I had gotten married a few months before and my husband worked in the daytime. We had moved to a rural town in St. Andrew, which made the commute to the hospital very difficult. The infrequency of the few buses that travelled to that part of Jamaica rendered the journey to and from home very difficult. While I was on night duty I spend most of the day travelling, so I was sleep deprived. I was granted temporary residence in the nurses' home and I was very happy to share a room with a student nurse. The student nurse also lived off campus and used the room in the nurses' home occasionally. I was very glad to be close to the hospital again and to get enough sleep. I worked three nights per week and I went home whenever I was off. Although I loved night duty, I could not wait to go back on days. When my night rotation was finished, I gave up my room in the nurses' home.

Chapter 10
From Staff Nurse to Midwife

Shortly after graduation I applied to the University Hospital of the West Indies School of Midwifery. I decided that I was going to do as many courses as I could so I also applied to do the Intensive Care Unit (ICU) course. I was still on night duty when I was called to the nursing office one morning and told that I was accepted into the midwifery program. I completed and returned the necessary paperwork and counted the days until I would begin training to become a midwife.

It was May 1984 when I started another phase in my journey as a nurse. The batch of pupil midwives consisted of about twenty-one staff nurses from different hospitals in Jamaica and one nurse from the Bahamas. I was still living in rural St. Andrew about twenty-five miles from the hospital, and after realizing the need to be close to the labor ward, I applied for a room in the nurses' home.

Early in the program my batch mates and I had to witness thirty deliveries before we could do any by ourselves. We were in the delivery room sometimes every evening and overnight on the weekends. We could not stay in the delivery room too late during the week because we had classes the next day. Sometimes some of the midwives on the labor ward called us in the nurses' home when deliveries were imminent. We abandoned whatever we were doing, including turning off the stove if we were cooking. One nurse was in such a hurry to run to the labor ward that she forgot to turn off the stove. Although her dinner was ruined she rejoiced because she witnessed more than one delivery that evening.

After many days in the labor ward, I finally witnessed thirty deliveries. I felt elated and was glad that I had accomplished this time-consuming task of witnessing thirty deliveries. Sometimes I stayed in the labor ward all night and witnessed no deliveries. I usually carried a book or my notes with me to study, but I found studying very difficult when the noise level in the labor ward was such that I wanted to be close to the laboring women in case they were about to give birth. I did not leave immediately after I observed deliveries but I helped in whatever way I could. I also had to document demographical information about all the deliveries I witnessed in my notebook. The documentation of the deliveries then had to be signed by the midwives who supervised the delivery.

The experiences in the antenatal clinic, the antenatal ward, the maternity ward, the labor ward, and the nursery were beyond my imagination. In the antenatal clinic I was assigned to different areas of the clinic. Sometimes I did blood pressures, tested urine for protein, weighed patients, or gave talks about conditions that were common in pregnancy to pregnant women before they were examined by the doctors or midwives. Registration of new patients was done about twice per week. We had to take all the patients' demographics and histories and make charts for them. The numbers of patients that we registered were entered in our notebooks and given to our instructors for evaluation before completion of the course. Computers were not used for registration, so everything was written by hand.

Some afternoons were spent preparing patients' charts for the next clinic visit. Gestational ages were calculated using pen and paper; although, calculation of gestational ages can be done with the aid of gestational wheels. Gestational wheels were not available for use therefore gestational ages were calculated by adding the number of weeks from the last menstrual period. We were not allowed to add the number of weeks from the last visit in case the calculations of the previous gestational ages were incorrect. We had to manually calculate the number of weeks from the last menstrual period for every clinic visit. I used gestational wheels for the first time in 1990 at a hospital in Brooklyn, NY.

The antepartum ward was a very interesting floor. The patients were in various stages of pregnancy with complications of pregnancy. It was on this ward that I learned about "kick count." Some patients had to report the number of times their fetuses moved for the day. If a woman reported less than ten kicks per day, other interventions were done: for example, sonogram or delivery of the fetus. I took great care in documenting the kick-counts on the kick charts, which were completed daily. I could hardly wait to be assigned to the labor ward. I monitored patients in labor, did vaginal examinations, and did deliveries with the supervision of midwives. My first delivery was uneventful, although I was very nervous. With the midwife's help, I did an episiotomy after giving the patient local anesthesia in her perineum. I also had to repair the episiotomy, which was also scary at first but got easier with subsequent ones. I had to scrub on three cesarean sections, and almost everything I did was recorded in the notebook I took to the labor ward with me every time I was on duty. Other duties were washing, and sterilizing instruments used for procedures done on the labor ward. Some of the tasks were similar to when I was a student nurse, such as weighing, bathing, and feeding babies. I also transported sick babies to the nursery and mothers and well babies to the maternity floor.

I learned a lot during the six weeks that I worked on the maternity floor. Every morning the patients took their babies to the nursery on the maternity ward. I examined the babies as I was taught by the midwives and instructed the mothers about the care of the babies as needed. I did "show baths" for new mothers (demonstration of bathing newborn babies) and took blood for bilirubin for babies who were or appeared jaundiced. My daily assignment on the 7 a.m. to 3 p.m. shift included giving discharge instructions to patients who were going home that day. The patients who needed home visits were sent to the domiciliary department to make appointments. The beds were washed and made by midwives, pupil midwives, and student nurses, and then it was time to admit the newly delivered patients who were waiting in the labor ward to come to the maternity ward. Most of the admissions were done on the noon to 8 p.m. shift. The admission process was made easy because there was an example of an admission package that was used for all patients. This was the easiest admission process of all the other wards that I was assigned.

Domiciliary was another exciting place to work. Visiting mothers in their homes was a very rewarding experience. The gratitude and the appreciation shown to the other nurses and I was very welcomed. Most of the patients were new mothers and mothers with medical conditions. Domiciliary was a change from the ward routine. In the mornings the midwives, other pupil midwives, and I packed the domiciliary bags with medical supplies that were to be used for mothers and their babies, reviewed the medical information of the patients that were to be visited that day, plotted our routes carefully to minimize travelling time, then boarded the hospital's van and began our visits.

The patients welcomed us into their homes. We assessed mothers and babies and educated the mothers as needed. We did several visits per day, but we had to get back to the hospital in the afternoons because appointments had to be made for discharged patients on the maternity ward. Sometimes there were increased numbers of patients to visit by the same number of midwives and pupil midwives and all the visits had to be made. I prayed that I made the right decisions as I instructed the mothers on the care of themselves and their babies when I visited them alone. It seemed that I did because there were no complaints. It was also the responsibility of the midwives and pupil midwives of domiciliary to assemble the charts in a specific order before they were sent to the medical records department. The time spent at the domiciliary department was rewarding. It was a new experience for me because this was the first time I was taking care of patients in their homes and I saw new places on the different routes. The only challenge

I had was writing the patient notes while the van was driving. Most of the progress notes had to be written before we got back to the hospital because other duties were waiting at the hospital and our shifts ended at 3 p.m.

My midwifery rotation took me through the family planning clinic. I learned the various methods of birth control and assisted clients in obtaining the birth control methods of their choice. It was the requirement of the midwifery course that all pupil midwives taught at least one childbirth class. I carefully prepared the topic that I was asked to present. My batch mates and I visited places that were relevant to our studies. For example, we visited the Department of Public Health when we were studying public health.

The eleven-month program ended with me doing a final paper on pyelonephritis in pregnancy. I chose that topic because my case study patient had pyelonephritis. The paper consisted of several pages and was hand-written. Typewriters and computers were not easily accessible. We also had to take the Nursing Council examination, which lasted two days. I had studied hard during the midwifery program, so I was not surprised by the results of the examination. The entire batch rejoiced, as we were all successful in the examination. Tears filled my eyes as I watched the graduation ceremony on the television. I did not attend my graduation because it conflicted with my day of worship. I hurried to the School of Midwifery the Monday of the following week and humbly collected my midwifery certificate, the award for being the most helpful student and some vouchers which I exchanged for books at the Liguanea Book Store in Kingston. My Midwifery Certificate had my name inscribed with beautifully carved letters and it added to my satisfaction of being a registered midwife.

Chapter II
Life Goes On

I looked forward to being assigned to one of the obstetric floors at the University Hospital of the West Indies, but that was not to be. I was re-assigned to the last ward I worked on before I started midwifery, but I was comforted because some of the nurses who I worked with before were still there. I worked as a staff nurse for about four months then I was summoned again to the nursing office. The long-awaited assignment had arrived. I was going to work on the maternity ward. I shared the good news with my coworkers and family and was thankful for the opportunity to work as a registered midwife.

The work on the maternity ward was the same as when I was a student nurse and a pupil midwife but now I had the added responsibility of mentoring student nurses and pupil midwives. It was sometimes challenging to work in charge as there were decisions to be made and there was no room for making wrong decisions. I was strengthened and supported by the ward sister who supervised the ward and the other midwives I worked with.

On the 12 p.m. to 8 p.m. shift I worked with a pupil midwife and a student nurse. The patients were admitted after deliveries or cesarean sections and they were discharged usually after an uneventful hospital stay. Two incidents stand out in my mind that reminded me that maternity nursing can be difficult. One evening when I was in charge, a patient who was alert and oriented started to bleed profusely and it was evident that she needed further intervention. Another patient was a doctor who I worked with before on another floor. She was transferred to the maternity ward after having a cesarean section. Shortly after being on the ward, she went into respiratory distress and had to be transferred to the intensive care unit for further management. I was the only midwife on the floor at that time, but the help that I received from the pupil midwife and student nurse was very valuable.

My first child was born while I was working on the maternity ward. Two of my coworkers and I gave birth a few weeks apart from each other. My prenatal care was uneventful except that I was very tired in the third trimester of the pregnancy. Getting ready for work was a struggle, and so I started maternity leave at thirty-six weeks, which was earlier than I had intended. My son was born via cesarean section four days before my due date. I decided early in my pregnancy that I wanted to have a cesarean section, but "patient choice" was not an option. I was elated when, at thirty-eight weeks of pregnancy, I was told by the obstetrician who evaluated me that my fetus was breech.

The news that I would be scheduled for cesarean section the next week was an answer to prayer. Having worked in labor and delivery at different times, I did not see myself going through labor pains. I had a strong desire to have children, but I did not want the pain that accompanied childbirth. I prayed constantly for God to create a reason for me to have a cesarean section, and He did.

I was admitted on the antepartum ward the day before surgery. I can remember the happiness I felt as I lay in the hospital bed and reflected on being a mother and taking care of my own baby. That evening I was transferred to the labor ward to make room for a pregnant patient who needed to be admitted. After all, I was just waiting for the next day to have my cesarean section. My preparation for the cesarean section began in the evening with my blood being drawn and the insertion of an intravenous line. I enjoyed my supper that evening knowing that I was not going to eat for a few days.

My son was born at 10:06 a.m. the following morning, and after recovering in the delivery room, I was transferred to the maternity ward, to be taken care of by some of my coworkers. The care I received on the maternity ward was outstanding. The seven days that I spent in the hospital as a patient made me reflect on the care that I gave to patients. I concluded that I worked to the best of my ability and I hoped that my patients were satisfied with the care that I gave to them.

My friends and some of my batch mates who were still working at the University Hospital visited me and cheered me up when I felt sad because my baby was sick and in the nursery. I gained much strength and encouragement from one of my batch mates who came from the Virgin Islands. She went back to the Virgin Islands after we graduated as staff nurses but returned to the University Hospital of the West Indies to do the operating room course. She visited me very often, and just reminiscing about our lives as student nurses was good therapy for me. Although I had worked in the nursery before, seeing my baby lying in a cot with intravenous fluid and a naso-gastric tube was very hard for me. The two months I spent at home with my baby were filled with joy. I wished that I could extend my maternity leave, but that was just wishful thinking. The month I took prior to the delivery of my baby shortened the time I had afterward. I did not regret starting my maternity leave early because I was very tired and I got all the rest that I needed.

I went to work in the antenatal clinic after my maternity leave because the hours of the clinic were more conducive to being a new mother. The other midwives and I managed the care of patients from when they registered in the clinic until they were twenty-eight weeks pregnant; they were only referred to the obstetricians if any unusual findings were detected. I had been working in the clinic for about nine months when I saw an advertisement for a childcare teacher in a secondary school in Kingston, Jamaica. I applied for the position because the hours of work per day were about five hours, which would give me a few more hours to spend with my baby.

In September 1987, I reported to work at the Edith Dalton James Secondary School in Kingston. The second of the two shifts enticed me more as it started at 12:15 p.m. Since I worked the afternoon shift, I had the mornings off to do whatever I wanted. I was living about twenty-five miles from work and because it was hard to travel by public transportation, I sometimes left home early in the mornings to guarantee that I was at work on time. I was arriving in Kingston several hours before work, so I enrolled in a sewing class to occupy my time. I learned to sew several types of clothes and felt accomplished as I wore the clothes I made. I also made clothes for my family and was very satisfied with my ability to sew.

The change from nursing at the bedside was welcomed. I enjoyed teaching and marking test papers. My sewing skills came in handy when I had to teach the students to make baby clothes. The clothes and other items made by the students were sold to the community, which brought in added revenue to the child care department of the school. My sojourn at the school was not for long because in January 1988, my family and I moved to Mandeville in the parish of Manchester. The change was very good for me because it was like going home. My mother was still living in Christiana, Manchester, which was about eighteen miles from Mandeville, and knowing that I was going to live closer to her was very exciting.

The journey from Kingston to Mandeville took about two and a half hours, and we were very happy to get to our temporary house. I was also very happy to get a temporary job at West Indies College, now renamed Northern Caribbean University. A more permanent house, which became our home for about one year and a half, was in close proximity to the university. I worked as a nursing instructor at West Indies College for a few months and then as Assistant Director of the Health Service for almost one year. All the students at the university had to be cleared by the Health Service every semester before they could register for classes. My duties included checking all the physicals and making sure they were up-to-date. I also rendered minor treatments and referred students to the doctor if necessary.

I looked forward to Fridays as my work day ended at mid-day. My work experience at West Indies College was enhanced by the spiritual atmosphere of the campus.

West Indies College offered a Bachelor of Science (BSN) nursing degree, and I took six credits per semester toward my BSN for three semesters and two summers. I will forever be indebted to the former West Indies College for affording me the opportunity to study at that great institution free of cost. I also enjoyed eating whole-some vegetarian meals in the cafeteria at West Indies College. In my quest to be healthier, I joined a gym in Mandeville. The cool Mandeville breeze was clean and refreshing as I inhaled it early in the mornings. Part of our routine at the gym was to climb a hill as fast as we could. While the gym instructor and others ran up the hill, I walked. But just the thought of being a member of a gym was an accomplishment for me.

I worked sometimes at Hargreaves Memorial Hospital in Mandeville and I was also one of the clin-ical instructors for nursing students from West Indies College who were doing their clinical rotation at the same hospital. I also worked as a registered midwife and as a staff nurse at Mandeville Public Hospital. I was happy to work at these hospitals since I got some clinical experience. Prior to moving to Mandeville, I was a child care teacher and had not worked regularly in a Hospital for about one year.

One night I was going to work at Mandeville Public Hospital when I had an unpleasant experience. I was walking on a street a short distance from my home and looking behind me to see if a taxi was coming in my direction. I saw a truck coming and I went very close to the road bank to give the truck as much of the road as was needed. As the truck passed, I was hit by objects in my face and chest. I used my hands to wipe my face to prevent liquid from going into my eyes. A taxi came shortly after and I was happy to go into it and be off the road. I was surprised when I got to work and realized that my white uniform had red spots with particles all over the front. I soon realize that I was hit with tomatoes thrown from the truck. I worked with a gown over my uniform that night and thanked the Lord that I was alive. I realized that I could have been hit with bigger objects or be shot with a gun.

One Sunday as I was looking through the newspaper, I lingered over an advertisement. It said that there would be a review class for all nurses who were interested in doing the Commission of Graduate Foreign Nursing Schools (CGFNS) examination. I was interested because I had studied on my own and taken that examination twice before and was not successful. I knew that I would benefit from this review class but how would I get to Kingston every day for a week was of great concern. I was living in Mandeville and working and studying at West Indies College. While I thought that it was possible for me to get vacation from work, I did not want to miss my classes.

After weighing my options, I took one week of vacation from work and made arrangements with one of my classmates to get the notes from the classes that I would miss. I went to a hotel in New Kingston the following Sunday and registered for the review course. New Kingston is a commercial area in Kingston, Jamaica, with many multi-storied buildings. The commute from

Mandeville to New Kingston was about two hours drive. I did not want to drive four hours daily so I spent the week in St. Andrew, an adjoining parish, where the commute to the hotel was about half an hour.

The review classes were very informative and prepared me adequately for the CGFNS examination. The numerous questions that were reviewed and the study tips given gave me the confidence and the skills I needed to do the examination for the third time. I thanked the Lord for putting Jamaican nurses in the recruiter's thoughts. The recruiter could have gone anywhere else in the world, but he chose to go to Jamaica, which gave me a chance to fulfill my dream of working as a nurse in the USA.

Chapter 12
Preparation

The study material that I took home with me kept me busy. I studied for the CGFNS examination as much as I could, and although I did not have a lot of time to study, I was confident that I was going to be successful. Working, attending classes, taking care of a toddler and studying for an international examination were overwhelming, but I made it through with the help of God.

The CGFNS examination was administered in a large lecture hall at the University of the West Indies. I was amazed to see the large number of nurses who were desirous of working in the USA. I was also in astonishment that my name was called first because my surname started with a T. I went inside the lecture hall and thanked God that I had more time to sit and relax before the examination started. I also realized that my maiden name was used because the first two times that I did the CGFNS, my surname was Ashley. The only place where my name appears as Paulette Ashley-Terrelonge is on my CGFNS certificate.

The examination had about three different sections and took several hours. I was relieved when I handed in my final paper and hoped that I would never have to do that examination again. The trip from Kingston to Mandeville afforded me time to reflect on the examination, and I felt calm and peaceful and was reassured that

I did my best. The review classes and the study materials that I was given on the final day of class prepared me adequately for the CGFNS examination. What happened next was totally up to the Lord and I was prepared to let the Lord do what He saw best.

I did not think about the results of the CGFNS examination for weeks. Then it came! I stared at the white envelope with the CGFNS logo then opened it. Words could not describe the way I felt after I saw the word "congratulations." I do not remember reading the letter in its entirety, but I started to wonder what it would be like to live in the United States of America. That letter was the gateway to a new life. After bringing my mind back to the present, I read the letter several times then I put it in a safe place.

The Sunday *Gleaner* brought another interesting piece of information. It said that all nurses who passed the CGFNS examination and were interested in working in the USA were to meet at a hotel in New Kingston. I made plans to go to this meeting, which turned out to be interviews for nurses. I was having my interview with the recruiter from Lutheran Medical Center when my two-year-old son ran out on the balcony of the hotel. I dashed to get him because he could have pushed himself through the rails on the balcony and fallen several floors to the ground. I completed the interview and application form with my son in my lap and was very happy when everything was over and we were free to leave.

Shortly after passing the CGFNS examination, my family and I moved to St. Andrew in Jamaica. I was reluctant to move at first because I did not want to risk missing a letter from the USA. I was reassured by the recruiter that my address would be updated. The three months that I was at my new home was very rewarding. I was able to be a "real mother" to my son. Although the time was short, I was a stay-at-home mom. Since I was expecting to migrate to the USA, I did not want to start a new job.

I was overjoyed when I read the letter from the recruiter stating that I was accepted to work at Lutheran Medical Center in Brooklyn, NY. I took the letter to the American Embassy in Kingston and was issued a H-1 visa, which granted me the privilege to work in the United States.

I stared at the airplane ticket that I received a few days later in the mail then realized that working in the United States was closer to becoming a reality. During the days that followed, I visited my mother and shared the exiting news with her and with all my friends. I went through my packed suitcases several times to make sure that I had everything that I wanted to carry to the USA. The hardest thing for me was to leave my son behind, but I told myself that I was going to make a better life for him.

During the final week before my departure to the US, I cleaned my house thoroughly and laundered all my son's clothes. The tiredness I felt at the end of each day was more than I bargained for, but knowing that I would not be doing those things for a while in that house brought some relief. I reflected on the home I would reside in the USA and wondered how the houses looked. Having not been to the US before nor having seen any picture of houses, I could only imagine.

Chapter 13
It's a Different World

Tears filled my eyes as I said goodbye to my son and all the other wonderful people that I was leaving behind in Jamaica. The trip to the airport was a very somber one. A few days before I had been very excited about going to the United States and now I wished that I did not have to go. I reflected on my life in Jamaica. As a little girl, my pastor's wife was a nurse who visited the United States sometimes. The gifts she gave me when she returned were very welcomed and were sometimes more beautiful than the things I had.

I remembered the applications I wrote to several hospitals in United States seeking employment. The frequent trips to the library at the University Hospital School of Nursing were rewarding academically because I was successful in all my courses, but the addresses I wrote out of the nursing journals did not help me to find a job in the United States. The third time that I did the CGFNS examination paid off. I was happy that I did not give up after failing the examination twice. One of the many lessons I learned was that if I didn't succeed on my first attempt, I must keep trying.

The route to the airport looked different and I started to miss the country that had been my home for thirty-one years. The uncertainty of when I would be travelling that route again made me very sad. The peninsula that housed the Norman Manley International Airport came into view along with airplanes that were landing and leaving the airport. As I passed the intersection that led to Port Royal, I reflected on the history that I learned about Port Royal and my visit there as a child. Port Royal was once the capital of Jamaica. More than half of Port Royal was destroyed in an earthquake in 1692 when the sea claimed more than half of the land that comprised the peninsula. The initial fear that I felt when I entered the Giddy House disappeared quickly as several people entered the lopsided building that was left on an angle after another earthquake in 1907.

The airport came into full view and soon I was at the departure terminal. With the check-in process completed, I was at liberty to walk around the airport. I was thrilled when I saw a nurse whom I knew. Her first name was the same as mine. We were student nurses together, but we were in different batches. I realized that we were going to work at the same hospital and I felt a little better.

The euphoric feeling that I felt as I entered the airplane was short-lived as I remembered that I was going to be in the air for several hours. This was the second time I was travelling in an airplane. My first airplane ride was about one year prior to this pending airplane ride when I visited Costa Rica in Central America. The difference was that I'd gone to Costa Rica for a visit but the trip to the US was a permanent one and I did not know when I was going to visit Jamaica again. Other nurses who were going to the same hospital were also on the airplane. Although I did not know all of them, we shared a similar goal and we bonded well on the airplane. The meal that I received on the airplane was very delicious and I consumed it with much satisfaction knowing that I would not have a meal prepared in Jamaica for a long time.

I believe that the twelve nurses who migrated to the United States on April 20, 1990 will always remember our trip to the United States and our quest to enhance our lives and that of our families. The aerial view of Newark airport in New Jersey and its surroundings was very beautiful. We arrived in the US in the night. The lights were bright and it was probably one of the most beautiful sights I had seen. I was happy to see the recruiter who picked us up at the airport. The trip from Newark airport to Brooklyn afforded me the opportunity of seeing the wide highways and the vast number of motor vehicles on the roads. We were taken to the first apartment and I indicated that I would like that apartment. I was also asked who I would like to share the apartment with and I indicated that I knew the other nurse with whom I shared a first name. As we entered the two-bedroom furnished apartment on the second floor of the red brick building, I exclaimed, "This apartment is beautiful." My roommate and I chose our rooms, which had similar furniture. My room only had two walls and it was between the living room and the dining room. There was food in the refrigerator and pots, plates, and utensils in the kitchen. I thanked the Lord for the opportunity of being in the United States as this was the desire of my heart since I was a student nurse.

My roommate and I had gone to nursing school together, and although we were in different batches and were not well-acquainted with each other in Jamaica, we shared the experience of migrating to the United

States together. We retired to our rooms after talking about ourselves and our families. The following day my roommate and I went for a walk around the neighborhood. The houses were built differently from those in Jamaica, and I was amazed to see the large number of cars that were parked on the streets. Our walk ended in a supermarket and I was astonished that the groceries that I bought only cost $9.00. I thought that those groceries would have cost much more. I forgot for a while that I was not in Jamaica where the currency is larger. It was much colder in NY than it was in Jamaica, but I was prepared for the weather. In the days that followed, the recruiters who planned our trips from Jamaica and took us to our apartments also took us to the social security office and to Lutheran Medical Center—the hospital that would be our employer. We lived in Sunset Park, Brooklyn, and our home was within walking distance from the hospital. The commute to the hospital took us through a shopping area in Brooklyn. This was to our advantage as we needed to purchase several items to make our new home more comfortable.

About one week after we arrived in the United States, we reported to work at Lutheran Medical Center. Orientation at the hospital lasted a few weeks and then we were assigned to clinical units. I was elated when I was told that I was assigned to labor and delivery as labor and delivery was my first choice of units. Orientation to labor and delivery lasted about three months. Although I had worked in labor and delivery in Jamaica, I had a lot to learn. I learned how to use the electronic fetal monitor because I auscultated fetal hearts with a funnel shaped instrument called Pinard Stethoscope in Jamaica.

In Jamaica, I titrated Pitocin by manually counting the drops, now I had to learn how to use intravenous pumps. I previously calculated gestational ages by adding the number of days since the last menstrual period, but now I used gestation wheels. I enjoyed using these new devices as they made my work easier. I also learned to scrub and circulate for cesarean sections. My experience with delivery by cesarean section was very limited and I only observed cesarean sections when I was a student nurse and pupil midwife in Jamaica.

I successfully completed my orientation and was assigned to work on the night shift. I was thrilled to learn that I was going to work three nights per week. On the first schedule, I was off for five consecutive nights, which afforded me enough time to visit my family in Jamaica. The work in labor and delivery was very exciting and my co-workers were very supportive. Some of my co-workers who worked on the day shift called me at home and got my order for supper, so that my supper was at work by the time I got there. My first Independence Day in the United States was well spent at a barbecue hosted by one of my co-workers. Some of my co-workers invited me to seminars, which were new experiences. One of the many conferences we attended took us from New York to Virginia. The experience of travelling on the Amtrak train was very exciting as we journeyed through the different states. We also went to other places of interest in Virginia including a water park. I was soaked during one of the rides, but it didn't bother me because I had a lot of fun.

I shared two apartments with my roommate. The second apartment had a washing machine and a dryer for our laundry needs. The second apartment was also different from our first apartment. In our second apartment, we occupied two floors. I also had the pleasure of sharing the second apartment with two additional nurses who were also recruited from the West Indies. One of the nurses was from Trinidad and one was from Jamaica. These two nurses moved out of the apartment after a short stay and we were back to the two original roommates who shared the same first name. After about one year of sharing an apartment with my roommate, we got our own apartments. I was living farther away from the hospital and my commute was mainly by taxi or bus. I walked to work sometimes when the weather was conducive to walking.

New Year's Eve in 1990 was a very exciting time at work. We all celebrated when my patient delivered at midnight. There were several patients in labor as I reported to work at 7 p.m. on New Year's Eve. I gave the usual care to the two patients that I was assigned, not knowing that one of my patients would be made into a celebrity. As midnight approached, and with her delivery being imminent, she was wheeled into the delivery room. With the help of the obstetrician, she delivered her baby at exactly midnight. This was a new experience, as I had not been afforded the opportunity to work in the delivery room on New Year's Eve before. I worked in the antepartum and postpartum wards and the antenatal clinic as a registered midwife in Jamaica. I received a telephone call from one of our union officers, who solicited information about the delivery. Within a few days, a representative from the union office came to the labor and delivery unit and took photographs of me holding the baby. An article with an account of the delivery and a photograph of me holding the baby were published in the nurses' union newsletter. It made me even happier to be working in the United States. I kept the newsletter for a few years, but it must have gotten thrown out as I packed to return to Jamaica in 1993.

One of the first challenges I faced in the United States was studying for and passing the state board examination. Keeping my job depended on the result of the state board examination. The one-year permit that I received from the Commission of Graduate Foreign Nursing Schools to work in the USA was not renewable. The one-week revision course that I took prepared me well because I passed the state board for registered nurse (RN). I also took and passed the state board examination for Licensed Practical Nurse (LPN) in case I did not pass the state board for RN, I could work as a LPN.

The passing of the state board examination for registered nurses made me very happy because my job was secured. Another reason was that my son, who was five years old, came to live with me. My babysitting needs were met in a few days after my son's arrival to the United States from Jamaica, and I realized that God had worked everything out. I was riding on a bus one day when I met a lady that I knew from Jamaica. She also knew my son and was willing to stay with him at night while I worked. This was an answer to prayer, as I did not have anyone to stay with my son while I went to work. Another answer to prayer came when I was looking for a school to send my son to. I did not have prior knowledge of the elementary schools where I lived so I relied on the yellow pages of the telephone directory.

After a brief look under schools in the telephone directory, I saw Hanson Place Elementary School. I enrolled
my son in that school and then my son and I started to
attend the Hanson Place Seventh-day Adventist Church,
the sponsor of the school. Six weeks after enrollment in
kindergarten, my son graduated. I was very excited to
be a parent of a graduate.

Chapter 14
Homeward Bound

I worked on night shift in labor and delivery for about three and a half years then a situation arose in Jamaica that required me to be in Jamaica. The leave of absence that I applied for was granted, so I started to make preparations to return to Jamaica. The process was tedious and was overwhelming. It did not require half as much of my energy and time when I was preparing to migrate to the US. I retained a shipping company that I found in the Yellow Pages of the telephone directory to ship my belongings to Jamaica.

I also found a storage company to store the things that I was leaving in Brooklyn. Regrettably, I sold the car that I'd bought a few months before. I was almost in tears when I was told by the car dealer how much the car was worth. I stared at the check in disbelief and wondered if I'd wasted my hard-earned money when I bought the new Honda Accord. The value of the car had depreciated, so it was worth only half of what I paid for it.

The day before my departure to Jamaica came very quickly. I wanted to go to Jamaica, but I was already missing my job and my friends that I would be leaving behind. My last day at work was three days before my scheduled departure from the US. I waited several hours for my landlord to collect the key for the apartment and return my security deposit on the day before my departure. The landlord did not come that evening, so I gave the key to one of the nurses that I came to the US with to give to him because it was getting late. That nurse lived on the second floor of the same building and she had occupied my apartment before. She told me about the apartment and I moved into it when she moved out. I was going to spend the night with one of my batch mates from nursing school who came to work in the US after I did. I bade my friends and neighbors goodbye, and my son and I took a taxi and headed for Queens. The taxi driver drove for hours and couldn't find my friend's address. It was after midnight, so I asked the taxi driver to take my son and I to a hotel. It took some time to find a hotel and by the time we checked into the hotel, I only had a few hours to get some sleep and to be at the airport at least two hours before my flight departing at about 7 a.m. With the check process completed, I was finally able to relax. I boarded the airplane and was happy to be going home.

I was happy to be back in Jamaica, and I wrote to the staff in labor and delivery at Lutheran Medical Center, inviting them to Jamaica. I enrolled in two nursing courses at Northern Caribbean University extension at Andrews Memorial Hospital. I was very happy to be studying again. One of the courses I did that semester was nursing research. My research topic was: "Does the Presence of Fathers in the Delivery Room have an Effect on Mothers' Perception of Pain?" The sample for my research consisted of nurses in labor and delivery and patients on the maternity ward at one of the hospitals I worked when I was in Jamaica. The research showed that the fathers' presence in the delivery room affected the mothers' perception of pain. Note-taking was very tedious, and I could not keep up with taking notes, so I enrolled in a shorthand class in a business school in Kingston for a short time. I did not use my shorthand writing skills because I returned to the United States before I completed the course. Since I did not practise writing in shorthand, I lost the ability to do so. I also worked in labor and delivery at the University Hospital of the West Indies one to two days per month.

During the semester, I received a telegram and opened it gingerly, fearing that something had happened to my mother. The telegram stated that my father was dead. With tears in my eyes, I fell on my knees and sought direction from God. In about two days, I left my home in Kingston and drove alone for about two and a half hours to my father's home in Christiana, Manchester. I was relieved when I got to my father's home because I had never driven that far before and some of the roads were narrow with deep bends. I thanked the Lord for taking me safely to Christiana, and I felt a sense of accomplishment. My greatest fear was that I would drive on the wrong side of the road. Motor vehicles drive on the left side of the road in Jamaica and I caught myself driving on the right side of the road and had to quickly move to my left. I travelled back to Kingston that same evening and as I neared my home, I was protected from an accident by my guardian angel who was my companion for the day. I made another trip to Manchester within a few days to attend my father's funeral. I was happy to see some of my cousins and other relatives that I had not seen for a long time.

The funeral was held in one of the churches that I attended as a child. The elementary school that I attended was named after the church. I also remembered the Christmas and Easter plays that were held in that church. I was not in the plays but I was usually in the choir. My graduation from secondary school was also held in that church.

I enjoyed my stay in Jamaica and so when the leave of absence that I took from Lutheran Medical Center expired I sent in a letter of resignation. Misfortune struck when, at the end of the spring semester, my car was stolen. I had parked my car in front of a hospital and gone to a nearby church. I was scheduled to work in labor and delivery that afternoon, so after church I hurried to the car. I stood in astonishment, as my car was not in the spot where I parked it. It must have been obvious that something was wrong, because a nurse who I met before detected it. I told her what happened and she helped me search the entire grounds around the church and the hospital, but my car was not found. As we searched for the car, more people found out what happened and were in awe that someone could steal a car from in front of a hospital and so close to a church, especially when service was in progress at the church. I informed the hospital what had happened and they were very sympathetic to my plight. After hours of searching, I gave up the search and walked to the Half-Way-Tree Police Station. I reported what happened and was reassured that everything would be done to find my car.

An angel must have accompanied me home because although the commute on the minivan was lonely, I maintained my composure and no one knew the turmoil that I felt inside. I went into my room and prayed earnestly that God would show me what to do. Within a few days, I decided to return to the United States. I had heard from a friend that my mother was not happy that I returned to Jamaica, so I was happy to visit her and tell her that I was returning to the United States.

Chapter 15
New Beginning

O n July 4, 1994, two days after my son's birthday, I boarded an airplane at Norman Manley Airport in Kingston, Jamaica, and headed for New York. I had mixed feelings because I left my family behind and I did not know where I was going to stay in Brooklyn. Nevertheless, I was happy to be going back to the United States. I had left some pieces of furniture in storage in Brooklyn, but I needed a temporary place to stay until I found an apartment.

The airplane landed in John F. Kennedy Airport in Queens and I left the airplane with the decision that I would go to the same hotel that I stayed the night prior to my return to Jamaica almost seven months before. My plans to return to Jamaica were shattered when the immigration officer told me that if I left the United States for the rest of the year, my green card would be revoked. That was the most devastating news that I had heard for a long time. I retrieved my luggage, went through customs uneventfully, then took a taxi to the Golden Gate Hotel in Brooklyn. I was relieved when I was told that there was a room since I did not have a reservation. The sounds of firecrackers reminded me that it was Independence Day in the United States.

I called some of my friends that night, one of which was my former roommate. The news I received from her was a direct answer to prayer. She said that she was going to Jamaica for two weeks and that I could stay in her apartment. Her flight was early the following morning, so I did not see her. Her landlord gave me the key, and then I went back to the hotel and checked out. Although I had to share my friend's apartment with a hamster and a cat, I was very grateful that I had a safe place to stay at least for two weeks. One day I opened the cage to feed the hamster and it jumped out. I was very worried that it would be eaten by the cat, so I searched the entire apartment and did not find the hamster. I did not want to spoil my friend's vacation so when she called from Jamaica, I did not tell her that the hamster was missing. After a few days of searching, I concluded that the cat had eaten the hamster. I went into the kitchen one morning to see the hamster on the kitchen counter. The Lord must have spoken to the hamster, because it did not run. Maybe it was very hungry and too weak to run. I put the hamster back in the cage and I subsequently opened the cage with caution.

I began searching for a job immediately. I called several hospitals in Brooklyn and was hired by Brookdale Hospital. My friend was scheduled to return to the United States in a few days, and so as not to inconvenience her, I moved to an apartment in close proximity to Brookdale Hospital.

My sojourn at Brookdale Hospital started on August 8, 1994. One evening after I returned home from orientation, I received a telephone call from Jamaica that baffled me. My car was found! The information that followed was not very pleasant and I was in a state of shock.

I was told that someone I knew stole my car and that the police found the car in his possession.

My plans to return to Jamaica were dismissed, so I sent for my son. Childcare was made easier with the help of my landlord, friends, and a day care which was conveniently located next door to my home. Due to the state of mind I was in and my inability to concentrate during orientation, doubt was created in my mind as to whether or not I would pass orientation. One day while I was on orientation, I mistakenly footprinted the left foot of a baby twice even though the footprint form indicated left foot and right foot. I corrected the error quickly, but because I was on orientation, I didn't think that the error would go unnoticed. It also took extra time to re-do the footprint correctly. I also remembered another time when I was scrubbing for a cesarean section, I had never seen suturing done with a straight needle. I used the needle holder to hold the needle and the remark made by the obstetrician made me leave the operating room immediately. After drying my tears, I regained my composure. I also dismissed the idea of quitting and allowed sound judgement to prevail. My fears of not passing orientation were allayed because I successfully completed orientation and I was put to work on the night shift.

The cold months approached, and I felt that I was prepared for the winter. Although I had on all that was necessary to protect me from the cold, I shivered at nights while I waited for the bus to go to work. I took taxis for a while, but it proved too expensive as I worked five nights per week. Sometimes I ran to the bus stop to catch the 11:10 pm bus, but other times I waited a long time at the bus stop. One night it snowed very hard that

I wondered how I was going to get to work. As I stood at the bus stop and thought that I did not want to be late for work, a Good Samaritan responded to my gesture for a ride and took me safely to work.

My manager must have seen potential in me because she offered me a position as an assistant head nurse. I refused at first, but then I thought of my finances and that this new position would give me an increase in salary. Six months after I started working at Brookdale Hospital, I became assistant head nurse on the night shift. The delivery room was very busy most nights and I often wondered if I would be able to do my job effectively. My fears were allayed as the years past. There were many nights when the nurses on duty were so busy, and just when we thought that we couldn't do anymore, other pregnant women came to the delivery room in various stages of labor. One very busy night stands out clearly in my mind. I was doing a delivery and one of my other patients needed antibiotics, so after the birth of the baby, I went and gave the patient her antibiotics then went back to the delivery. Sometimes I had four actively laboring patients who had to be assessed every fifteen minutes and there was no central monitoring. By the time I finished attending to the fourth patient, it was time to go back to the first patient. And the cycle continued.

Chapter 16
From Diploma to BSN

In my quest for further education, I applied to the City University of New York. It took about two years to meet all the requirements, so when I received a letter that I was accepted in the nursing program at Medgar Evers College, I was elated. In the fall semester of 1995, I started my journey to complete my BSN degree. I was thankful for the credits that I received from University Hospital of the West Indies School of Nursing and West Indies College which counted toward the 128 credits that I needed to complete my BSN degree.

The four years I spent at Medgar Evers College were not easy. I did at least six credits every semester, and sometimes I left work and went directly to classes after some busy nights at work. I also worked per diem at Franklin Hospital in Valley Stream. During my second semester at Medgar Evers College I also passed the inpatient obstetrics examination.

As I started the nursing courses, I needed to get every Wednesday off. Sometimes I had clinicals all day on Wednesdays and nursing lectures in the evenings. Wednesday was a well-chosen day since very few people were off on that day. I did not encounter any problem with getting the day off for college. Most of my vacation time was used to attend college as I used vacation days on many of those Wednesdays. Physical assessment was especially challenging to me. Assessing the different body parts in the proper sequence and using the right terminology was not easy. My batch mates and I utilized the nursing laboratory to the fullest by practising physical assessments on each other frequently.

The final exam came and although I practised physical assessments thoroughly, I was very nervous and very relieved when I passed the course. I enjoyed my community health classes and clinicals. It was one full day every week. I did home visits in the days, had classes in the evenings, and then went to work at nights. I worked on nights so I got Tuesday nights off, but I had to work on Wednesday nights. My shift started at 11:55 p.m. Twelve-hour shifts were not an option for me because I could not get to work by 8 p.m. on the evenings that I had classes. Therefore, I worked eight-hour shifts five nights per week.

In January 1998, I seized the opportunity to go to England with other nursing students and a professor from Medgar Evers College. We spent six days in London, England during which time we visited St. Thomas' Hospital and Florence Nightingale Museum. It was with a sense of humility and disbelief that I entered the Florence Nightingale Museum. I had learned about Florence Nightingale, the lady with the lamp, in nursing school, and I had recited the Florence Nightingale pledge many times. The visit to the Florence Nightingale Museum almost twenty years later was a very fulfilling experience.

We also visited other places of interest such as Buckingham Palace. I was moved by the compassion and love that were demonstrated by the English people.

It was about five months after the death of Princess Diana, but the large number of flowers that were placed at the palace gate made it seem as if she had just died. One day my foot ached badly from walking around London. I leaned on a shelf in a store and, to my dismay, the shelf and all its contents fell to the floor. I bent down to pick up the pieces of broken glasses when someone said that it was "okay." I left the store rejoicing that I did not have to pay for the broken items. It was a dream come true to be in England because England was my motherland. Although Jamaica gained its independence from England in 1962 many Jamaicans still visit or live in England.

The one-day trip that my roommate and I took to Paris from England was very inspiring. I had seen pictures of the Eiffel Tower in Paris, but to be in close proximity to it was awesome. The parts of Paris that I saw were very beautiful. The tour guide explained the different places that we went and, although my time spent in Paris was short, I learned enough about Paris to make my visit worthwhile.

I admired the terrain of the town we visited. As I stood on a hill and looked down at the beautiful homes in the valley, I reflected on the many hills that I journeyed over in Jamaica. I often went up the hills one way and went down another way. I enjoyed the breathtaking view until the van drove back down the hill. The train rides to and from Paris were very fast, which gave us more time to spend in Paris. The enjoyable trip to England and Paris came to an end and soon the group and I were on our way back to the USA.

I was elated when I was informed that my name would appear in the 63rd volume of *Who's Who Among Students in American Universities and Colleges*. I maintained a 4.0 GPA for the first two years at Medgar Evers College. I cried when I received a grade of C for pathophysiology in my third year of college. I went to the professor and hoped that there was a mistake, but there was none. Prior to that class, I had received A's for all my courses. I received an A+ in both statistics and sociology. Statistics was done in the first semester and sociology was done in the second semester. The fifth semester started out on a wrong note for me. I missed the first pathophysiology class because I had to do a microbiology examination so that I would not have to do the microbiology course. I did not attend the third class because I went to Jamaica to attend the funeral of my late nurse manager. The first pathophysiology test was the following week. I did not study because I did not know about the test. It was no surprise that I did not do well on the test. Although I did not get the grade I wanted, I learned valuable, life-changing information. On the advice of the professor of pathophysiology, I only bought brown sugar and took 1000 mg of Vitamin C every day for many years.

I usually took one course in the summer, but during my final summer, I did two courses because I wanted to graduate the following May. Although tiring, I attended classes six hours per day Monday through Thursday every week for six weeks. I was especially impressed with one of the two classes. It was an advanced literature class in which the class was required to study "Masterpiece Literature." The first book we studied was the book of Luke from the Bible. I was also exposed to the arts because the class attended a ballet performance at Lincoln Center in New York.

The well-anticipated graduation came. As my name was called, I walked briskly to the podium and, after having my photograph taken with the college president, thankfully accepted my degree. The rays of the sun pelted down on me, but it did not seem to bother any of the graduates because we sat outdoors for the duration of the graduation on a sunny day in June 1999. I was very pleased to be a BSN graduate of Medgar Evers College. My batch mates and I celebrated, as it was obvious that our hard work had paid off. I received my official degree in a black leather-bound binder a few days after graduation, and the words "magna cum laude" were inscribed under my name. This increased my sense of achievement. I thanked the Lord, because I always prayed for knowledge, wisdom, and understanding.

Chapter 17
From BSN to MSN

I was looking through the *Nursing Spectrum*, when I saw an advertisement for an open house at Long Island University in Brooklyn. *Nursing Spectrum* was a magazine with information on nursing and career opportunities that I received in the mail every month. I immediately decided that I would like to further my studies so one evening after my management clinical at Saint Mary's Hospital, I attended the open house. There were two obstacles to overcome that afternoon, but I was determined to attend the open house on time. I had a flat tire, and since I did not know how to change a tire, I went searching for a tire shop. I was thankful that my tire was fixed and soon I was on my way to Long Island University. The other obstacle was that I could not find parking. Long Island University is located downtown Brooklyn where parking is difficult. After circling the university several times, I saw someone pulled out of a spot and I gladly pulled into the spot. I was thankful that I persevered and went to the open house because the information that was presented was valuable and I left Long Island University determined to be a nurse practitioner.

I applied to the University and was invited to attend an interview at the University. I worked the night before the interview, so that morning I hurried home to get some sleep. I was awakened by lightning and thunder, but I knew that I had to go to the interview. I prayed and got ready for the interview and then the rain stopped. Lightning must have struck my house because some of my appliances that were working that morning were not working after the thunderstorm. I hurried out of the house in an effort to attend the interview on time and hoped that the thunderstorm would not affect my mother who was visiting from Jamaica.

In September 1999, I started my journey to become a nurse practitioner at Long Island University in Brooklyn, NY. I felt a sense of achievement knowing that I was studying for a master's degree. I matriculated as a part-time adult nurse practitioner student. Classes were in the evenings, so I was able to get a few hours of sleep before I went to class and one to two hours of sleep before I went to work at 11:55 p.m. I was very happy that I passed the two courses that I took every semester because I did not want to repeat any classes. The work was hard, but I depended on God to take me through.

The most challenging part for me was to meet the requirement of 300 clinical hours. I did the first hundred hours with my primary care physician whose busy practice allowed me to gain some experience of evaluating patients with a variety of medical conditions. Working on the night shift allowed me the time I needed to do clinicals about two days per week. I also had to spend my time making more frequent visits to my obstetrician because I was pregnant. At about twenty weeks of pregnancy I could hardly walk because the growing uterus was pressing on a nerve and I was in severe pain when I tried to move. I was not able to work for about three weeks and I ambulated with a cane. I was not able to do clinicals, but I went to some of my classes.

One evening I went to class and the pain was so bad that I must have taken four times the usual time to walk from the parking lot to my classroom. I made it to class a little late and I sat gingerly at my desk and tried hard to find a comfortable position but could not. The two-hour class seemed longer than usual but it was finally over. I asked a batch mate to assist me in standing, but she must have thought I was pretending to be in pain because she refused to help me. I struggled to get up from the chair and, with the aid of my walking cane, I walked slowly to the parking lot. The journey home was not a pleasant one because I was in pain, especially when I had to press the brakes, which I could not avoid because of the frequent traffic lights.

After about three weeks I went back to work and I resumed my clinical hours with my primary care physician. I continued until the end of that semester. Determined not to fall behind because I was pregnant, I did a four-week summer course when I was about eight months pregnant. The course was very interesting, and the teacher was dynamic. A group of us went to see the congressman for our district as was assigned by our nursing professor. This visit was a very fulfilling experience and something that I would not have done had it not been for that class.

I was very relieved when the course was finished and thankful that my pregnancy was uneventful during the course. I was scheduled for a cesarean section on July 30, 2001, so I pre-registered for my courses for the following semester, knowing that I wouldn't have time after the baby was born. My daughter was born via cesarean section and I was privileged to be cared for by the staff that I worked with for several years. I took six months maternity leave and, although I had no income after two months, the time spent with my daughter was very rewarding.

In September 2001, Long Island University started a family nurse practitioner program, so I switched from the adult nurse practitioner program to the family nurse practitioner program. The ten additional credits that I had to take went by very quickly as they were taken in one semester. I was happy to make the switch from adult nurse practitioner to family nurse practitioner because I thought that I would be more marketable. I also used a part of my maternity leave to complete my required clinical hours.

On September 11, 2001, I was doing clinicals in the family planning clinic at Kings County Hospital when news went through the clinic that an airplane crashed into the World Trade Center in Manhattan, NY. Other staff members and I rushed to a television in the waiting area of the clinic. I was in disbelief as I watched the television and saw what happened. I thought that this was a horrible accident, but when a second airplane hit the other tower, I was in shock.

The remainder of the day was very somber. The other nurse practitioners and I saw the patients who were waiting to be seen, and at the end of the day I drove cautiously home and was relieved that I got home safely. Classes were cancelled at Long Island University for that day. The weeks that followed were hard for me because the topic of regular conversations was that many people were killed in the World Trade Center.

The experience I gained in the women's health, family planning, medical, and pediatric clinics at Kings County Hospital was very valuable. Some days I spent the entire day at the clinics, attend classes in the evenings, took care of my baby when I got home, and then went to work at nights. I did all my clinicals in about four semesters and I was relieved when I completed the required number of hours. Sometimes I did my homework or studied with my baby in my arms. My mother, who had come from Jamaica to help me, had returned home a few days before the attack on the World Trade Center. My mother had looked forward to going home and had she stayed in the United States for a few more days, she would have had difficulty getting a flight to Jamaica.

My hard work paid off because I became a member of the Lambda Iota Upsilon Honor Society at Long Island University. I received my master's of science degree in nursing and thanked God for making it possible. I did not know about master's degrees until after I became a nurse and I did not think it would be possible for me to have one. The graduation was held under a tent and as I listened to the ceremony and all the different programs that were called, I felt very honored to be a graduate of Long Island University.

Chapter 18
Post MSN

I resigned myself to continue to work as a registered nurse. The numerous applications I sent out to work as a nurse practitioner were unanswered. I had a ray of hope after attending three interviews that I would be accepted for one of those positions. I was offered a job as a nurse practitioner and was saddened when the job offer was withdrawn. I enjoyed working as a nurse in labor and delivery, so I continued with that job. I wanted to work on the day shift but there were no available day positions. My daughter, who was almost two years old, did not sleep in the days, so I could not sleep either. The two to three hours of sleep that I got in the evenings was not enough to allow me to function at my maximum capacity. I resigned from the job that I had with no offer of another job. During the last few nights at my job, I received the pleasant news that Jamaica Hospital Home Care Agency was hiring nurses. I had wanted to work in home care because of the rich experience that I gained during the semester I spent doing home care while attending Medgar Evers College. Rendering care to patients in their homes and being outdoors for part of the day was one of the reasons I liked the flexibility of being a nurse.

Jamaica Hospital Home Care Agency afforded me the privilege of fulfilling my dream of being a home care nurse. I felt as if I did my best to help patients in their homes. My aim was to make a difference in the lives of the patients I visited. Some patients went to their doctors for treatment because I advised them to do so. I witnessed patients make lifestyle changes, deep wounds heal, and patients get well. One of my patients stood out in my mind because I witnessed a miraculous wound healing.

As I received the paperwork for my new patient, I stared at it in unbelief. The prescribed treatment for the patient was "Dressing change twice daily and pour 100 percent pure honey into wound." I visited the patient and after doing my usual greeting, we sat around her dining table and completed the paperwork. I assessed her wound and wondered why the doctor prescribed that line of treatment. I had never heard or seen honey applied to wounds. Nevertheless, I followed the doctor's instruction.

I dressed the wound twice per day for about one month and saw the wound got smaller and smaller. I went to do the dressing one day and, to my amazement, the deep wound was completely healed. Tears filled my eyes as I bade the patient farewell. Home care was very rewarding but there were also a few downsides. I went to visit a patient one day for a scheduled visit. I rang the bell relentlessly for a long time and I called her number with no answer. It was then I realized that the loss of electricity in some boroughs of New York City for about one week, rendered her doorbell and telephone inactive. Sometimes, I couldn't find the addresses of the patients because I didn't know the neighborhoods. I did not have Global Position System (GPS) and it seemed as if

I had problems following the directions that were given to me. I was disappointed when I received a parking ticket although sometimes I put a sheet of paper with the words "Visiting Nurse" on the dashboard of my car. Sometimes, I drove around for a long time looking for parking, thus shortening the time I had for the visits or prolonging my days.

I worked in home care for about one year, but then the longing to work full time in a hospital grew very strong so I went to work in obstetrics at Franklin Hospital Medical Center in Valley Stream. While I was at Franklin Hospital, I became Advanced Cardiac Life Support (ACLS) certified for the first time. ACLS was a requirement for working in labor and delivery (L&D) because we had to aid in the recovery of patients who had surgical procedures such as cesarean sections. Franklin Hospital afforded me the opportunity of working on day and night shifts in L&D, nursery, and postpartum. I also worked in the women's health center in the years that I worked per diem at the hospital.

Franklin Hospital was a great place to work. The staff was helpful and caring, and the atmosphere was serene and beautiful. Living in Brooklyn and driving to Long Island to work was relaxing for me. I was profoundly saddened when I was told that the obstetrics unit was going to be closed at Franklin Hospital. I had to face the reality that I would have to work in another area of the hospital or leave Franklin Hospital. The only other area of nursing that I wanted to work in at Franklin Hospital was the emergency department. I was disappointed when I was not accepted to work in the emergency department. I was offered a full-time position at Victory Memorial

Hospital in Brooklyn where I was working per diem, but I decided to work in labor and delivery at Forest Hills Hospital in Queens, which was closer to my home and a part of the health system that I was already working for. I never saw myself as a manager, so when I was offered a job as a patient care manager, I declined at first but then accepted, knowing that I could do all things through Christ who gave me strength.

The fear I had of working as a patient care manager quickly subsided because it was similar to the job I did for eight years as an assistant head nurse in labor and delivery at Brookdale Hospital. The added duties were managing postpartum and nursery and doing payroll. There were some mornings that I was happy that I arrived home safely. The blowing of horns reminded me that I was not in my bed. Opening my car windows even in the winter did not seem to prevent me from falling asleep, especially at the stop lights. The night shift started at 7 p.m. and ended at 7 a.m. then I had to take my daughter to school. Sometimes the only time I sat was after I left work, so I was very exhausted after work.

I did night shift for seven months and then I was asked to work on the day shift. It was a challenge to leave work at 4 p.m. Although my daughter was in an after-school program at her school until 6 p.m., I still managed to accrue late fees. One day I did not leave work until after 7 p.m., so I asked my daughter's babysitter to pick her up from school, but she forgot. My daughter was at school until about 8 p.m. I was very grateful to my daughter's teacher for staying with my daughter so the least that I could do was to take the teacher to her home so that she would not have to take the bus. I also thanked the Lord for enabling me to send my daughter to that private school because if it was some other school, I would have had to pick my daughter up at the police station.

It was a usual work day, but the information that I got when I logged onto my computer changed my life. I read the email that stated that the health system of which the hospital I was working for was a part of, had been given a grant and that the grant would be used to pay for nurse practitioners and other advanced practice nurses to pursue doctorate degrees in nursing practice at Case Western Reserve University. I did not hesitate but replied to the email immediately and indicated my interest. I was told how to apply, so I printed the application form from the university's website and looked it over carefully, noting all the requirements. I mailed the completed application along with my resume and an essay in which I wrote about my educational and professional goals and my research interest. I was also required to send in my midwifery diploma although I had done midwifery more than twenty years before in Jamaica. I had to search for my diploma and was relieved when I found it. I was happy that I did not leave it in Jamaica because had I done that, I might not have been accepted to pursue a Doctor of Nursing Practice degree.

My trips to Medgar Evers College and Long Island University, my alma maters, were two-fold. I requested my transcripts and references from three of my former professors. The Lord supernaturally gave me the time to go on these errands. My regular shift was 8 a.m. to 4 p.m. Monday to Friday, which were the hours when the offices are open at the college and university. When my boss asked me to work 3 p.m. to 11 p.m. on two consecutive evenings, I thanked the Lord for making the time available for me to apply for my transcripts and my references. Some months later I was informed by Case Western that they had only received two of my references. After contacting about three different professors, one consented to giving me the reference, but I had to send her my transcript from Medgar Evers College, where she taught me and my photograph. I happily sent them to her because she was going to help me meet the requirements so that I could start my doctorate degree. I was expecting a phone call from Case Western, so when the phone rang, I picked it up with great expectations. The interview with one of the professors at the University left me wondering whether or not, I was going to be accepted, but I was elated as I read the acceptance letter. I did not hesitate to mail in my response, and I looked forward to the day when I would have my first class.

Chapter 19
A New Era

By the time I figured out how to access the online course that I registered for, it was too late to buy the required textbooks. I read as much as I could of the readings that were online. Then, in about two days, I was on a train to Connecticut, as a hotel in Connecticut was the venue for my first class. There were about fifteen students in that class, one of whom was the nurse manager who hired me at Franklin Hospital in 1997. This was now March 2007 and we were students together. The course was six days long with three days each week for two weeks. The two different trips that I made to Connecticut were worth the investment into my education. I did not concentrate on the difficulty that I had in getting home the second week. The trains were re-routed, and I had to take about four different trains and waited a long time between trains. I got home very late and had to prepare for work the following morning.

The course was very informative, and the discussions were very enlightening. The professor also told us about Case Western Reserve University, which was exciting to me because I did not get to read much about the university on the website. I borrowed a textbook from my professor and read a few chapters one night until I realized that I'd used the same book in my nurse practitioner program. The book was not packed away too far, so I found it with ease at the bottom of my bookshelf. The book was like new. The course was not as difficult as I expected. I thought the courses in a doctorate program were supposed to be hard.

The hotel room was comfortable, and the staff was very accommodating. The staff came to my aid when I needed a microwave in my room. I had brought some food with me that could be prepared in a microwave. I also had some of my meals at the hotel. Some of my batch mates and the professor stayed at the same hotel, so we lingered a little longer in the conference room after classes and talked to each other.

After the six days of classes—which were held on Fridays, Saturdays, and Sundays for two weeks—I took the train back to New York and pondered over the course I just did. The class was given take-home assignments that were due at different times throughout the semester. My assignments were done early in the mornings between 1 a.m. and 3 a.m. and on Sundays. At the end of that course I was rewarded with a grade of A.

I looked forward to my next course because it was held on the campus of Case Western Reserve University in Cleveland, Ohio. On Mother's Day 2007 I waited at the airport for what seemed to be an eternity. The flight was delayed in hourly intervals until it finally left the airport about eight hours after the scheduled departure time. I had booked a room on campus but since I arrived in Cleveland after midnight, I did not think that I would find anyone on campus, so I decided to stay in a hotel overnight. The patient taxi driver took me to three different hotels and I booked into the third one. I was happy to be in a room and went promptly to bed because I wanted to get some sleep so that I could stay awake for my all-day class in a few hours.

The following morning, I took a taxi to the Frances Payne Bolton School of Nursing at Case Western Reserve University. That class was bigger than the last one and I did not know anyone in the class. The course was for six consecutive days and during that time I got to know all the students. The class was divided into groups of about four students each. My group, the daffodils, spent several hours preparing our project, which we presented on the sixth day. I was more prepared for this course because I had all the required textbooks and I'd read more of the required reading before the course started. On the evening of the first day, I went to the hotel and checked out and was happy to move into my room on campus. My dormitory room was quiet and reminded me of the nurses' home in Jamaica. There were two bunk beds, a closet and a table in the room. The bathroom was at the end of the hall and there was a kitchen that everyone on that floor used. My neighbors were nurses from the health system, one of which was the nurse executive for the hospital where I worked.

Living on campus was fun for me. One evening I went to a yoga class at the gym on campus. I had done yoga regularly in the past but the demands of working as a manager gave me no time to do that activity. I ate most of my meals in the cafeteria of the hospital on campus. Case Western Reserve campus is very big, and my room was not close to the classroom. All the other nurses who lived in the dormitory were doing different courses, so I walked to my classes alone.

I had put my suitcase on the bottom bunk, but since I was not going to climb to the top bunk to sleep, I pulled the mattress down to the floor. I slept on the floor for the six nights that I spent on campus. There was no television or radio in my room, so Three Angels Broadcasting Network (3ABN) was my company. 3ABN is a Seventh-day Adventist television station that I enjoyed watching in my spare time. I had brought my computer and USB cord with me and I was happy to find an Internet outlet in my room. I also did some modules of a fetal monitoring course that I was required to take online.

I was moved to tears after attending a graduation ceremony at Case Western. This graduation was held on my last day on campus. I was overjoyed and felt very privileged to attend the nursing graduation held at a church near the campus. Graduations for different departments at Case Western were held at different venues. I was a bit uneasy at the graduation. I was mindful of the time and wondered when to leave so that I would not be late for my flight back to New York. I slipped out quietly through a side door of the church after all the graduates received their degrees. I left the graduation ceremony with a determination to complete the DNP program so that I could graduate one day. My suitcase and other pieces of luggage were heavy, but I finally made it to the train station where I boarded a train to the airport. On the way to the airport my eyes were fixed on the scenery of Ohio, something that I was deprived of on my arrival. I had arrived in Ohio after midnight and all I saw were the numerous traffic and motor vehicle lights on my way to the hotel.

As the train approached the airport, I wondered how difficult it was going to be for me to carry my luggage to the check-in point at the airport. I was relieved when I found out that all I had to do was take the elevator to the second floor. After my suitcase was checked in, I went to get something to eat. I was also doing a statistics course online. Since it had been more than ten years since I did my last statistics course, I was required to do a basic statistics course. I was very happy and relieved that I found a suitable course online, since I did not think I had the time to go into a classroom. This course was not offered at Case Western and it had to be done before I could do advance statistics. I had taken my statistics book to Ohio, but I did not get to do much classwork. By the time I got to New York, I studied most of the chapters of the book that I was required to read for that week.

The next course I did was at the same hotel in Connecticut where the first course was done. This time I did not stay at the hotel but drove from New York daily for classes. The first morning I left my home early, which turned out to be a very good thing because I went the wrong way about three times. I did not have GPS at that time. I was very relieved when I parked my car in the parking lot of the hotel and made it to my class on time. The six days were divided in two but this time there were two weeks between day three and day four. In this class, I formulated my research topic and was very excited that I was nearer to completing the DNP program.

The two weeks of vacation that I took in January 2008 were well spent. I went to St. Kitts for the other two courses that I did. I changed planes in Puerto Rico and, although I did not leave the airport, I was happy that I was in another territory of the US. Puerto Rico also shared something in common with my place of birth. They were both located in the Caribbean. The classes were very interesting, and the environment was very different. The guesthouse that I stayed in overlooked the Caribbean Sea, and sometimes I watched the ships as they entered and left the harbor. Some of the classes were held in the nursing school, which was not far from the guesthouse. The nursing school also overlooked the Caribbean Sea. We were transported to the school by a faithful bus driver who also took the group anywhere we wanted to go.

Although I went to St. Kitts to study, I had time for fun. I took a boat to a nearby island called Nevis with four other nurses. We had breakfast at one of the hotels in Nevis, shopped in some of the boutiques, and spent the remainder of the day by the sea. A delicious lunch was prepared for us in a shop by the sea. After a well-spent day, we took the last boat back to St. Kitts. The boat ride was enjoyable and being on the Caribbean Sea brought back a lot of pleasant memories. The Caribbean Sea also surrounds Jamaica, where I was born. As I settled in my bed that night, I thought of the events of the day and thanked God for creating those beautiful islands.

One of the many places of interest that I went to in St. Kitts was a place where the Caribbean Sea and the Atlantic Ocean met. The difference in those bodies of water was very obvious. The Caribbean Sea was calmer than the Atlantic Ocean. Some of my classmates stayed at the Marriot Hotel, which gave me reason to visit my classmates and enjoy some of the facilities of that beautiful hotel, and was privileged to walk on the shores of the Atlantic Ocean. The cuisines of the different restaurants in St. Kitts were delightful and very delicious.

My portrayal of a woman who owned a small clothing business by the Atlantic Ocean outside the Marriot Hotel was well received by the class. This was a very fitting character for me because I was the only one in the class who looked like the people from St. Kitts. This presentation was done as a requirement of one of the courses to present the organizational structure of a business. My group members and I were excited and satisfied that we performed a skit that made our presentation different from the others.

The two weeks in St. Kitts went by quickly, and soon it was time to bid farewell to all. Our final group gathering was at another wonderful restaurant where we had a hat party. This was a good social event and I was awarded a prize for being the most patriotic. As I boarded the small airplane back to Puerto Rico, I could only reflect on the goodness of God and that He has the whole world in His hands. I was also grateful that the quest for higher education took me to places that I might not otherwise have gone.

Chapter 20
The Change of Events

It was Nurses Week in May 2008. The excitement of the events that were planned for the week made me feel very happy that I was a nurse. But, the enjoyment of the week was not to be. On May 5, 2008, the first day of Nurses Week, the new car that I'd had for only six months was totaled. I was driving through the last intersection before I arrived at my coworker's home when another car hit my car. I was very shocked and in disbelief as this was my first accident. The traffic light was still green and then I realized that the other driver ran through a red light. I tried to stay calm but my co-worker who was sitting in the front passenger seat started to scream, and my daughter, who was in her booster seat behind me, started to cry. I was thankful that there were no visible injuries on my daughter who was six years old. She stopped crying after I put her into my lap, so I concluded that she was just scared.

The air bag on the steering wheel in my car was deployed and there was broken glasses all around me. The window of the door on the driver's side was broken and the door was badly damaged. I thanked the Lord that the three of us had our seat belts on and there were no visible injuries on any of us. The ambulance and the police came and, after opening my door with much difficulty, we were taken to the emergency room of the closest hospital. While I was in the emergency room a policeman gave me a ticket because he did not find the registration for my car. The pain of receiving the ticket was more than the pain I felt from my injuries. My co-worker, my daughter, and I were evaluated by different doctors and released from the hospital. As I entered my home that night I was thankful to God for sparing our lives and that none of us had to be admitted to the hospital that night.

The following day a good Samaritan took my daughter and I on several errands. I first went to the pharmacy to get the pain medication that was prescribed at the hospital the night before. Then I was taken to see the car and was shocked to see the extent of the damage. I was escorted from the car into the waiting ambulance after the accident, so I did see all the damages that were done to my car. I was then taken to a rental car company, where I rented a car. I drove behind the good Samaritan who took my daughter and I to a medical complex.

I completed some paper work and waited to be seen by the doctor. I hurried to the door as my name was called and was disappointed to learn that there was no doctor in the facility. I went into an office and was introduced to a chiropractor. I told the chiropractor that I did not need his service and left. I drove home in the rented car and was thankful that I did not succumb to the injuries that I received from the accident. I was resting at home when I was called by the good Samaritan and reprimanded for leaving the medical facility.

My primary care physician had moved from his office across the street from my home and I didn't have his new address. I searched the yellow pages and found a doctor near to my home. He gave me a referral to a hospital in Queens, NY to do a computerized axial tomography (CAT scan). I drove a long way to the hospital and was happy to reach my destination amidst the obstacles. This was the first time I was going to that hospital, so when I got to a major road that I was told would take me to the hospital, I was relieved. Fear gripped me as I stared at the sea of cars on the road below and before me. I soon realized that a major highway had divided the road. I was directed how to get to the other side of the highway and was relieved when I pulled up in front of the hospital. Another obstacle was that I could not find parking. I didn't want to park too far from the hospital because it was night and I didn't know how long I would have to wait at the hospital. My daughter and I spend several hours in the hospital and just when I thought that I was going to be discharged, I was told that my hemogloblin was very low and I needed to be admitted. I looked at my daughter who was sleeping on the stretcher beside me and refused to be admitted. I signed out against medical advice and left the hospital. It was 3 a.m. when I got home. I thanked the Lord for taking me on this adventurous journey and went to bed.

I visited the doctor about two times in three days and each time my hemoglobin was done. When I saw that my hemoglobin was lower than the previous two times after the accident, I consented to be admitted. I was happy that all the tests I did at the hospital came back negative and that I did not need to have surgery. I felt very lonely in the hospital and concluded that the lack of visitors was because the hospital was far away from many of my friends. The company of the hospital staff was very welcome. The only other visitors I had were my son and a co-worker. I did not receive many calls because the telephone in my room did not always work.

I studied statistics as much as I could in the daytime. I lay awake at nights wanting to study but dared not turn the light on for fear that I disturbed my roommates. I was in a two-bed room, but in four days I had three different roommates. I looked forward to my meals since I selected them. It was in the hospital that I learned that my car was totaled. On day four I asked my doctor if he could discharge me and he did. My son drove me home, and as I neared my home, I decided that the first thing I would do was to go for my daughter who was staying at her babysitter's home.

I began to scream as I listened to the messages on my answering machine. There were several messages that said my mother was dead. After gaining my composure I called my stepfather in Jamaica and he said that my mother died on May 16 and he had been trying to contact me since. My mother died two days before I was discharged from the hospital. I flopped into a chair and sobbed profusely. I thanked the Lord again that I did not need to have surgery because if I did, I would be in the hospital longer and I might have missed my mother's funeral.

I was alone at home and, with much difficulty, planned what I needed to do. I called my son and the lady who kept my daughter while I was in the hospital. I also informed my boss that I was out of the hospital and that I needed to go to Jamaica the following day. I managed to book flights for my son and I and then I drove to the home of the lady who kept my daughter. I was very grateful that she consented to keep my daughter until I returned from Jamaica. I did not want to take her out of school since she had already missed two days of school after the accident. My daughter had missed a state test, which her teacher allowed her to make up when she returned to school. My daughter complained of pain in her left shoulder after the accident, but she told her doctor that she had no pain. I was very concerned about her since she was sitting behind me and the car was hit on our side.

I was having pain in my left side, left elbow, and left knee and I took painkillers regularly in the hospital, but with the news of my mother's death, my physical pain was insignificant. I had started on online statistics course and assignments were due twice per week. Due to my hospitalization, I was behind on my assignments. There was no time for sleep because after I finished doing my assignments and packing, it was time to go to the airport for the first flight I could get to Jamaica. The flight was early the following morning.

I emailed my statistics professor about my circum-stances, and I asked my son to email her again informing her that I was on my way to the airport. As the airplane lifted off the ground at John F. Kennedy airport, my spirit lifted because I enjoyed travelling in airplanes. I always love to go to Jamaica, but under the circum-stance, I wished I didn't have to go. While I waited for my connecting flight in Miami airport, I called some of my co-workers and told them what happened and where I was going.

My mind was in turmoil as I waited for the second plane to leave for Jamaica. I usually take non-stop flights to Jamaica but, as this flight was the first one to Jamaica, I had to take it.

Chapter 21
The Dark Days

I usually love to go to Jamaica, but there have been some instances when I wished that I didn't have to go. I went to Jamaica to attend three funerals of people I loved dearly and whose lives have impacted me in positive ways. I was in a state of grief when one of my batch mates from Batch 82 died in May 1996. This was one of my closest friends in nursing school and we shared the same first name. She called me about three weeks before her death and I rejoiced with her on the birth of her second son. I told her that I would visit her at her home in Queens in about two days since I thought that she would be home by then. The following day I received a telephone call from her husband who told me that my batch mate was in the intensive care unit. I visited her in a hospital in Manhattan and was shocked to see her on a respirator. I prayed that she would get well soon, but her work on earth must have been done because she never left the intensive care unit but died three weeks after she had her baby. I represented Batch 82 at the funeral in Jamaica and visited her family in New York for about six years.

One of the nurse managers who hired me and whom I worked with for many years also died and the funeral was in Jamaica. I was saddened to learn of her illness. I visited her at her home and also in another hospital in

Manhattan. Her death spread quickly through the hospital and I made plans to go to Jamaica. After attending these funerals, I visited my mother in Jamaica so I could have some time to redirect my attention before I returned to the US. The two funerals were in Westmoreland, one of the parishes in the west of the island. The third funeral was that of my mother. I did not have anywhere else to go but had to remain at my mother's home for the duration of time that I would be in Jamaica for her funeral, so my heart was heavier as I boarded the airplane.

As the airplane landed in Jamaica, I said a prayer and the fear that I felt before was instantly lifted. I felt calm and was reassured that I was not alone. I rented a car at the airport and my son drove for more than three hours to my mother's home in Christiana. There were a few obstacles along the way. We were stopped by a policeman who said my son was speeding. I told him our mission in Jamaica and he had compassion on us and did not give us a ticket. We took the policeman's advice and drove at a slower pace for the remainder of the journey. I was always taken home by someone who'd lived in Jamaica and knew the roads very well, so I did not pay much attention to changes that had been made to the roads since I'd migrated to the USA. The directions that I gave to my son took us on a very adventurous trip, which was good because I was able to see more of Jamaica.

As the car pulled up in front of my mother's house, my heart started to beat faster and I felt very nervous. I reluctantly got out of the car and one of the first people I saw was my stepfather. He filled me in on some of the details of my mother's death and I was surprised at how well I kept up. I thought that I would break down and cry, but then I realized that I had to be strong for the others. The mood at my mother's home was very somber, but I was encouraged by the many people who came to visit daily.

As I looked at my mother lying on a table in the funeral home, I remembered the last time I saw her, and how well she looked. But now, she was gone. Selecting a casket for my mother was very hard, but with the help of my stepfather, I selected a very beautiful one. After leaving the funeral home we went to the hospital where my mother died to apply for the death certificate. I began to reminisce because I was walking in the same corridors that my mother must have walked with me as a baby. I was in the hospital where I was born. It was also at that hospital that I did the entrance examination to become a practical nurse and where I was given the address to University Hospital of the West Indies School of Nursing where I was trained to be a registered nurse.

I wondered what it would be like to work in the hospital of my birth as a registered nurse. I had planned to go back to my mother's home and work at that hospital after I completed my training to be a registered nurse, but my plan was aborted in my final year as a student nurse. I saw some nurses walking along the corridors and I thought that I would rather be in a hospital working than being there to apply for a death certificate. I was brought back from daydreaming as my stepfather approached and said that he would have to return to the hospital the following day to get the death certificate.

I was happy that I did not have to drive that day for fear that I might have an accident. I could not concentrate very well, and I might have driven on the right side of the road as I was accustomed to doing in the US. Motor vehicles drive on the left side of the road in Jamaica. We finally arrived home and found that some friends of my mother came to visit. They remembered me although I had not seen them since I was a child.

The days that followed found me making arrangements for the funeral. I had to make another trip to the funeral home but this time I went alone. My son went to visit his cousins in another parish. I left my home early in the morning and arrived at the funeral home safely. I was very thankful to God for protecting me on the road, which was narrow and had many bends. I stopped on the road several times to allow motor vehicles going in the opposite direction to pass as I did not think that the road was wide enough to allow two motor vehicles to pass each other freely.

With the funeral expenses paid and the clothes that my mother was to be buried in delivered to the funeral home, I was ready to drive the eighteen miles back to my mother's home. I was thankful that a night shift worker at the funeral home was going home and drove with me a part of the way because navigating the road was easier at his advice. As I pulled into a parking spot in a parking lot in Christiana, not very far from my mother's home, I was surprised when a gentleman told me that I had a flat tire. I must have driven too close to the bank of the road because I remembered that I quickly righted the car and I was very frightened when the car ran off the road and into the stony road bank. The kind gentleman offered to change the tire for me, and he entrusted me with the care of his baby.

The following day the rental car company came and changed the tire, so I now had four good tires on the car and a spare one. With the funeral arrangements made, the car was not driven until I was returning to the USA. On my final day in Jamaica, my son drove most of the way to the airport. I was relieved when my son finished eating so that he could take over the driving of the car from me. I don't know if it was the effects of the accident I'd had about three weeks prior to my mother's death, but the few miles that I drove felt like eternity.

I was very contented to be in the passenger's seat. The trip to the airport was shorter than the trip from the airport one week before. This time my son's cousin met us on the outskirts of Kingston and we drove behind his car to the airport. With the check-in process completed, I went to the departure gate and was alone after many days. My son went back with his cousin as he was spending some extra time in Jamaica. My mother's house had people coming in and out every day and night, and by the time the last set of people left for the night, I was so tired that I "passed out" in the bed.

I played the events of the previous days in my head and I was surprised at how strong I was. Of all my siblings, I was the closest one to my mother. I made all the funeral arrangements, so I was happy that my mother was laid to rest uneventfully. I wondered if the attendance to the funeral would have been better if it was on a weekend instead of a Monday afternoon or if it was because the band played all night on the night before the funeral. When I was a child in Jamaica, people went to the homes of the dead and sang, but the singing by neighbors and friends had been replaced by bands.

Chapter 22
Role Reversal

I have heard many times that nurses make some of the worst patients. I don't know if it is true, but I will tell you my story and you can form your own opinion. I have been hospitalized five times. My first hospitalization was in 1985 after I had a miscarriage. I was elated when I found out that I was pregnant, but my happiness tuned into sorrow about three months later. I was at home one day when I started to have excruciating abdominal pain. The pain medication that I took rendered no relief, so I had no choice but to go to the hospital. I remember thinking that the timing was so wrong. Couldn't it be on a day when I was at work? It would be so much easier, I thought. Two neighbors took me to the same hospital that I was working in, which was about twenty-five miles away. The commute to the hospital was very difficult although I had travelled that same route many times before. I screamed every time the car went into a pothole because the pain was worst then. I was happy to be on a stretcher and in the emergency room. Seeing some familiar faces calmed me a bit, but soon I started to scream in pain. I was promptly given an injection with pain medication. The needle was hardly out of my gluteus maximus muscle when I started to get some relief from the pain. I was admitted on the ante-partum ward and once the pain was gone, I slept soundly.

I was awakening by severe abdominal pain and rang my bell to summon the nurse. A nurse who I worked with before promptly administered an injection of pethidine and soon I felt relief. Pethidine was one of the most potent analgesic drugs used for pain relief. I administered the same medication to many of my patients in my nursing career. The following morning, I was informed by a doctor that I had lost the pregnancy and that I was scheduled for a dilation and curettage to remove the remaining products of conception. After regaining my composure from crying, I signed the consent form for the procedure and was taken to the Minor Operating Theatre for the D&C as it was called. I reflected on the many times that I pushed patients in stretchers along those same corridors to the Minor Operating Theatre to have similar procedures. Having had the procedure, I slept for a while and then I was discharged.

My second hospitalization was in 1986 when I was scheduled for a cesarean section. I had packed all the items that I needed and went to the hospital the day before the cesarean section. I was a little apprehensive, but I was happy that the pregnancy was coming to an end. I later realized that I was not taking the iron tablets as I should. I took them once per day instead of three times per day as was written on the container containing the iron tablets. I suffered the consequence by starting maternity leave one month earlier because I was very tired. Having arrived at the hospital, I was assisted to the antepartum ward where I was admitted and assigned to a two-bed room. I had just settled in when I was told by a doctor that I was going to be transferred to the delivery ward. I was relieved when I was told that there was no problem with my fetus, but that my bed was needed for another antepartum patient. I was happy to go to the delivery room where the preparation for the cesarean section started. A scar on the dorsal area of my left hand reminded me of the pain I felt when the intravenous line was being inserted. After a good night's sleep, I was awakened early in the morning to continue the preparation. I could hardly retain the enema, which was required before elective cesarean sections in those days. Soon all the preparations were done, and I waited anxiously behind the curtain that separated my bed from the others.

My son was born via cesarean section at 10:06 a.m. After recovery in the recovery area in the delivery room, I was taken to the maternity floor. I had very good experiences during my seven-day stay on the maternity floor. I was told by the obstetrician who did the cesarean section that some bleeding was seen on my bladder, so I had to keep the Foley catheter in for seven days. The Foley catheter was very convenient because it afforded me the luxury of not having to go to the bathroom to urinate. It was difficult for me to walk to the bathroom at the end of the corridor and I did not want to use the bedpan. On about the third day after the cesarean section, I was very hungry, and I was still having water in graduated amounts. I could not take the hunger anymore, and so I pulled out the intravenous line. My plot was successful because I was given a full cup of peppermint tea shortly after. The intravenous line was not reinserted and I was given a light meal that evening. I had a full meal for breakfast the following morning, which I thoroughly enjoyed. I was discharged on day seven and I was very sad to leave my baby behind. The kind pediatrician said that I was to go home and come back for my baby the next day. I took his advice reluctantly and when I got home, my neighbor asked me for the baby and I sensed that something was different. It was not usual for a mother to go home without her newborn baby, but I did.

My third admission was for my second scheduled cesarean section in 2001. My obstetrician decided early in my pregnancy to perform a repeat cesarean section because she did not have any information about my first cesarean section that was done in Jamaica fifteen years earlier. I thought how different it would be to deliver my baby in a hospital in which I was not known by any of the staff, and so I chose my obstetrician because she was affiliated with another hospital. One night when I was about twenty-four weeks pregnant, I went to the labor and delivery room for preterm contractions. I was given two liters of intravenous fluid then I was discharged after a few hours. I was very compliant and did not utter a word that I was a nurse who worked in labor and delivery in another hospital.

As destiny would have it, my doctor moved back to the hospital where I was working and where I had worked with her before. I had no recourse but to consent to deliver my daughter at that hospital and in the delivery room where I was the assistant head nurse at nights. I was reassured by one of my co-workers who pointed out that it was better to give birth in a hospital where I was known. That co-worker stayed back after her shift so there was an extra pair of hands to assist with the cesarean section.

On the morning of the cesarean section, I went to the hospital about 6 a.m. where one of my coworkers on the night shift prepared me for the cesarean section. The insertion of the Foley catheter was very uncomfortable, and the placement of the epidural was painful. I had general anesthesia with my previous cesarean section and the Foley catheter was inserted after I was anesthetized.

My fourth admission was during Nurses Week 2008. As was mentioned before, I had a motor vehicle accident on my way home from work on the first day of Nurses Week. I was discharged from the emergency room of the nearest hospital. After a few days, my doctor sent me to a different hospital for a CAT scan, and it was also discovered that my hemoglobin was low. My doctor recommended that I be admitted, but I signed myself out of the hospital against medical advice. I was very concerned when my hemoglobin, taken at three different times, was lower than the previous time. At the advice of my doctor and my son, who was a student nurse and who had come home from college for the summer break, I decided to be admitted. My son took me to the hospital my doctor was affiliated with and I was admitted and assigned to a two-bed room. I was alone in the room for a few hours, but the other bed was soon occupied by another patient. The following morning, I refused the basin of water that was put on the bedside table and requested to have a shower. My request was granted but I was not happy with the appearance of the bathroom. I used the basin for the remaining three mornings that I spent in the hospital, concluding that my hygienic needs were met better at my bedside.

Some of the procedures done were a blood transfusion, colonoscopy, and an examination by a gynecologist. I also experienced the loneliness of being in a hospital. I wanted to do my statistics homework but could not because I needed to use the Internet, which was not available to me in the hospital. I was also missing my daughter whom I had not seen since admission because the hospital was far from the home where she was staying. I requested to be discharged on the morning of the fourth day when my doctor came to visit me. My request was granted, and I got a little inpatient as I waited for the discharge papers. The timing of my discharge was perfect as within a few minutes of being home I was making plans to go to Jamaica to funeralize my mother.

My fifth and final admission was in 2012. It was the Christmas break and I was looking forward to spending time with my daughter, who was out of school. My grandson, who was three months old, was going to be spending some time with me. I had my Christmas break all planned, but my plans were not to be. I was trying desperately to get rid of a cough, so when one of my friends gave me a remedy that she said would stop my coughing, I did not hesitate to use it. I cut a head of garlic, a piece of onion, and an orange into small pieces and boiled them. I drank about half cup of the concoction three times for the day as I was advised to do. As a nurse you would have thought I should know better, but I learned the hard way. I used too much garlic and I was fasting the same day and didn't eat until in the afternoon. The cough continued, and I took some cough syrup before going to bed that night.

I was still coughing the following morning, so I took some more cough syrup. I went on a prayer line (a conference line that is mostly used for prayer), as was my custom, and I was kneeling and praying when I felt light-headed and fell to the floor. I tried to get up and then I fell again. My children called the ambulance, but by the time the ambulance came I was revived. I think the garlic lowered my blood pressure. My son took me to the emergency room of the hospital where he worked. I was admitted and had several tests done, all of which were negative. I spent about five days in the hospital, and on New Year's Day 2013, I requested to be discharged. Several hours passed and I did not see the doctor who I was told was coming to see me, so I signed myself out against medical advice. I wanted to go to work the following day, which was the beginning of a new term at school.

Chapter 23
The Open Doors

As a child, I went to Sunday school in Jamaica and learned many songs including one that said, "I am the door, I am the door, by me if any man enter in, he shall be saved, he shall be saved, he shall be saved." I went through that door and was saved and my life has never been the same since. I was about seven years old when I made the decision to be a nurse. God must have inspired me to make that decision because no one in my family was a nurse.

I was not an eligible candidate for the common entrance examination (a national examination that determines placement into high school) because one of the requirements for doing that examination was attendance of extra lessons, which I did not do because my mother could not afford to pay for extra lessons. Another opportunity came for me to do the grade nine achievement test. I was overjoyed the day when the results were released. I was not only happy that I passed the examination but also for the appearance of my name in the national newspaper, *Gleaner*. I kept that page of the *Gleaner* with my name in it for many years.

The first night after the results of the examination were posted was a sleepless night for me. It rained heavily that night and I remembered hearing the raindrops on the rooftop and wondering when the rain would stop. A song that I learned at church played repeatedly in my mind. It said, "The windows of heaven are open, and the blessings are falling tonight. It's joy in my heart since Jesus made everything bright." My future looked bright because I was going to attend one of the best high schools in Jamaica. It was summer vacation, so I could not contact my classmates; telephones were not available in many homes as they are today. The members of the young people's group at my church were the first to know of my success. God opened the door for me to attend Holmwood Technical High School.

I attended Holmwood Technical High School in Christiana, Jamaica, for three years and then the door to Knox Community College was opened to me. I needed two more O-level subjects to get into nursing school. I was the only one pursuing my course of study at Knox Community College where a program of study was designed for me. One day a friend at college said that she had some problems, but at eighteen years old I said I did not have any problems. Looking back, I know that I could honestly say that I did not have any problems because the Lord was with me.

Another door was opened when I was accepted to study nursing at University Hospital of the West Indies. It was a childhood dream of mine to become a nurse and God turned this dream into a reality. Another dream was to be a midwife, and the door was opened for me to do midwifery. After working as a staff nurse, a midwife, a childcare teacher, a nursing instructor and an assistant director of health services, the door was opened for me to migrate to the USA.

Doors opened for me to be an assistant head nurse of a busy labor and delivery in a hospital in Brooklyn, New York. With God's help, I had that position for eight and a half years. I resigned from that job and worked as a registered nurse on an obstetrical floor at a hospital in Valley Stream, NY, rotating through labor and delivery, maternity, and the nursery. Another door was opened when that hospital closed its obstetrical unit. I applied for a job as a labor and delivery nurse at another hospital, and during the interview, I was offered a position of a patient care manager of labor and delivery, maternity, and nursery. I questioned myself as to whether or not I could do that job, but I was reminded that I could do all things through Christ who gave me strength. This was a familiar verse in the Bible that I learned as a child and which propelled me along when I thought that I could not do a task. God also prepared me for this managerial role because I faithfully completed my assignments where ever I was assigned when I worked at the hospital that closed its obstetrics department. The thirteen twelve-hour shifts per months had equal assignments to work in labor and delivery, nursery, or postpartum. I did not complain but was happy for the opportunity.

Educational doors were also opened. I completed my bachelor's degree in nursing (BSN) and graduated magna cum laude from Medgar Evers College in Brooklyn. At Long Island University, I was on the honor roll and humbly graduated with a master's degree in nursing and as a family nurse practitioner.

I thought that I had achieved all my educational goals, but then doors were opened for me to enroll in a doctor of nursing practice program at Case Western

Reserve University in Cleveland, Ohio. My educational journey at Case Western took me to Cleveland four times, Connecticut four times, and St Kitts in the West Indies once.

When I was in Jamaica, I wanted to become a public health nurse, but I migrated to the United States before this dream became a reality. After I was terminated from the position as an assistant nurse manager, God opened the door for me to work as a school nurse. The termination of my position as an assistant nurse manager was a blessing in disguise. I usually extended myself to meet the needs of the hospitals for which I worked. But this time, I had to put my daughter first. I couldn't do night duty at the time when I was told that doing night duty was my only option. I had become a single parent and my son was attending college in another State. I did not have anyone to stay with my daughter at nights and so I did what I thought was the "motherly" thing to do. I decided to stay home with my daughter until I acquired a job with more convenient hours. I called my boss and resigned verbally, and I received the termination letter about three months later. The ten months that I was a stay-at-home mom was very rewarding. I took my daughter to and from school every day, went to the library and park with her, attended parent – teachers meetings, and more. Tears filled my eyes as I watched my daughter received her award for one of the students of the month. I concluded that I made the right decision to leave the job as an assistant nurse manager. The job title was changed from patient care manager to assistant nurse manager. No amount of money could replace the joy I felt in spending time with my daughter.

I accepted a number from a friend who had started to work as a school nurse a few months prior. The number was for her supervisor who gave me the number for the nurse recruiter. I applied for a position as a school nurse and was offered a position of a public health nurse without having gone to public health school. Being the holder of a Bachelor's Degree qualified me to be called a public health nurse. More than seven years later, I still enjoy working in a school. The time spent with my daughter, who is now in high school, and my two grandchildren is very rewarding.

These experiences taught me valuable lessons. I learned that God placed me where I needed to be at every stage of my life and that no one can shut a door that was opened by God or open a door that God closed.

Chapter 24
The Opportune Time

W hile I was doing my BSN degree, I passed the inpatient obstetric examination. Having failed that examination twice before, the Lord impressed upon me the need to take it again after many years. With less time to study than the two previous times, I questioned myself as to the reason and the benefit of taking that examination again. The two courses that I was taking toward my BSN were more than enough work. Plus, I was working full time. I made time to study for this examination and passed it. My courses were not affected because I received A's for both courses.

As I held the newborn babies in labor and delivery and the nursery, I could not help but wanting children of my own. My beautiful son was born two years after I graduated as a midwife. Joy filled my life as I watched this precious child achieve his milestones. He was such a perfect child, but I thought that he would benefit from having another child to play with. Having grown up as an only child, I knew how boring it was at home, especially during the long summer holidays. My dream of having another child was fulfilled fifteen years later. After my daughter was born, I was thrilled to see how caring my son was to his sister. My children did not grow up together because by the time my daughter was two years old my son went away to college. My son returned home after four years and has significantly contributed to his sister's and my welfare. My children were born in God's own time and I am reaping the blessings.

I questioned when I was going to finish the doctorate degree that I started and was working on so enthusiastically. Within the first two years, I had completed twenty-one credits. One more credit was done in the following year, but the remaining six credits seemed to take forever to complete. To God be the glory, after a long break I was motivated to continue where I left off and after ten years, I graduated from Case Western Reserve University with a doctorate degree in nursing practice. I was reassured that God would work everything out in His time and He did.

I did not drive a car for about four and a half years. I did not have any desire to drive after the accident I was involved in that totaled my new car and could have taken my life. The buses and trains took me where I needed to go with very little hassle. Every time winter came around, I wished that I had an alternative to walking in the snow or waiting at the bus stop. Four winters passed and as the fifth winter approached, I felt the need to buy a car. God provided the money to buy a car. God was also with me because I felt so comfortable driving that it was as if the four and a half years that I did not drive were erased.

I was very impressed with my new license plates and I thought that the letters and numbers meant something. The license plate number was "GDP 1874." Within a short time I came up with an acronym for GDP: God Deserves Praises. But I could not figure out 1874, which looked like a date. I looked up 1874 on the Internet but did not find anything significant. This date was also not heard of by a friend who remarked that if it was 1844, I would not have to think too hard because 1844 is very significant in prophecy. My conclusion was that God Deserves Praises 1,874-plus times.

I had discontinued my cell phone for about two years after someone texted me a negative message. Like the car, I told myself that I did not need a cell phone. I had all my conversations at home and my children had my work number in case of emergency. My daughter started to attend junior high school and I bought her a cell phone as she was going to commute by public transportation and I needed to communicate with her to ensure that she arrived at school safely. I also activated my phone, and my new number ended with 8174. This was about three months before I bought my car. So with the license number being so close to my telephone number, I thought that this had to mean something. I have not found the meaning as yet.

Before I bought the car, I told the Lord that I would use it for His service. The Lord has helped me to keep my word because many people have benefited from the use of my car. My prayer partner who helped me to pray for the car was one of the first recipients of the use of the car. She was moving, so for two evenings after I left work I headed to her old apartment. We loaded the car as much as we could, and after several trips, we managed to move everything except the items that were too big to fit into the car. I also used the car to collect several items of clothing and shoes to take on mission trips.

Many events have happened in my life that made me realized that there is a time for everything. Several opportunities have seemingly passed me by, but I believed that the right time came when these opportunities came again some years later. I also believe that everyone will achieve their destiny if they keep their goals in sight.

Chapter 25
Against All Odds

G od has been really good to me and I know that all I have achieved and the person I have become are evidences of God's hands in my life. I have had some struggles in my life, but they only made me into a stronger and more determined person. I live each day with total dependency on God. Prayer is the weapon that I use to overcome all obstacles. I usually do not make any decisions without consulting God in prayer. I have struggled to pass some examinations or attain certain goals that I thought would have been beneficial to my life, but God has allowed me to be victorious against all odds. I was dumbfounded when I was told by the examiner that I did not pass the driving test. This was the second time I was hearing those words. I spent hours learning to drive and even my driving instructor was surprised that I failed the road test again. One of the hardest things for me to do was to inform the Toyota car dealer that I had failed the road test again. I don't know what had gotten into me or what I was thinking, but I bought a car before I had a driver's license. The Toyota dealers kept the car for me until I received my driver's license. I thought my previous experience of driving in Jamaica, although limited, would help me in obtaining a driver's license in the US.

I returned to New York with a sense of accomplishment and great satisfaction. In August 1992 while I was vacationing in Florida, I passed the road test, so I got a Florida driver's license. I was doing a one-week review course for the inpatient obstetrics examination and was not able to pick up the car, so I asked a friend to pick it up for me. My Toyota Corolla was well needed because I was on night duty and I had to rush from work to take my son to school in the mornings. Finding parking on the busy streets of Brooklyn was very difficult sometimes. One morning I was very tired after a busy night at work. The drive around several blocks searching for parking proved futile. Feeling very tired and sleepy I parked before a supermarket. I was almost sure that I would get a parking ticket, but two tickets were more than I bargained for. I took the two tickets that were stuck between the wiper blades and the windshield and slumped into the driver's seat of my car. As I drove to pick my son up from school, thoughts of having to pay two parking tickets would not leave my mind. It was late in the afternoon and some parking spots were available by the time I returned home. I was happy to find a parking spot close to my home because I went to work in a few hours and I didn't have to walk too far in the night.

If it was not one thing it was another. One morning I was happy to find parking near to my home, so I parked my car and went to bed. After stopping the alarm clock, I jumped out of bed and hurriedly got dressed. With just enough time to pick up my son from school, I picked up the car keys and my pocketbook and hurried out of my apartment. I stared at my car and wondered how I was going to pick my son up from school. It was a

Friday and my son's school was dismissed earlier on Fridays than other school days. My car was blocked in and there was no way out. There was no parking on the other side of the street during cleaning of the street, so a car was double parked beside mine; one car was before and one behind. I had to resort to taking the train to my son's school.

Sometimes I forgot that I was pursuing a doctorate degree in nursing practice (DNP). In 2007, the thought of doing a terminal degree sounded good to me. I enrolled in Case Western Reserve University where the program of study seemed to fit my schedule. The final two courses were done in St. Kitts, and as I travelled back to the US, I felt a sense of accomplishment. I hoped that within the next year I would have done my project and be ready for graduation. This was not to be, because five years later I was at the same place academically as I was when I left St. Kitts. I tried desperately to do my project, but I met with several obstacles. I have had two committee chairs. The first chairperson was my advisor in the DNP program. I took so long to complete the program that she retired before I was done. The second chairperson was one of my committee members. She also taught me Research I. It was in her class that I formulated the topic for my research project.

I was happy to return to Case Western Reserve University in Ohio to do Advance Research Part II. The six days of intense classwork sometimes felt like more than I could handle, but I persevered. I taped all the lectures and was determined to pass the course as I did not want to repeat it. I returned to New York feeling very overwhelmed and wondered where to start. The class was given assignments, and the first one was to do a codebook for my proposed project. My luggage that was intentionally left in Ohio by the airline was a blessing in disguise. All my course material was in that piece of luggage. So that night I was able to relax, and I was thankful for a good night's sleep.

The luggage was delivered to my home the following morning and my head started to pound as I removed the contents from the suitcase. As I reviewed the coursework and the material of how to make a codebook, I thought that making a codebook was one of the hardest thing that I ever had to do. I prayed and asked God to show me what to do. I reviewed the material again and it became as clear as crystal. I did the codebook and mailed it to my professor in Ohio before the deadline. The Lord increased my understanding in such a way that I was able to explain the assignment to another classmate.

Chapter 26
Reinstated

I started the doctor of nursing practice program in the spring semester of 2007 and completed all my coursework by the end of 2008. The defense for my first proposal, titled, "The effect of aromatherapy on the perception of pain in women in labor," was successfully completed in 2010. I was elated when I defended and passed that milestone in my journey to complete my degree. I submitted an application to the Institutional Review Board (IRB), which was located in another hospital of the health system by which I was employed. I was working on the obstetrical unit and was desirous of doing the project in the labor and delivery unit. Disappointment was an understatement for the way I felt after learning that my proposal was deferred. I did not do any further work on my proposal for over one year because I could not fulfill the recommendations made by the IRB.

One day I received an email from one of my committee members who later became my committee chair. She encouraged me to continue and not to give up. She encouraged me to modify the research topic, which I did. The revised proposal was to determine pregnant women's knowledge of aromatherapy for pain relief during labor. The revision took a few months, during which time I looked for a site for data collection. I no longer worked in the hospital where I had hoped to conduct the study. I contacted numerous places to do my project, but I was denied.

A few years passed and then the same committee member who encouraged me before, advised me to modify my research topic again, which I did. The third revision of my proposal was to determine nurse-midwives' knowledge and use of aromatherapy for pain relief during labor in the United States. I went on the Case Western Reserve University website to register for the next semester but was not able to log in to my account. After consulting the help desk, I realized that I had been dropped from the DNP program. I then remembered that I was told that I had seven years to complete the program. I was in the seventh year and I had not register for about four years, or eight semesters.

I wrote a letter to the director of the DNP program explaining the obstacles I faced and expressing my desire to continue the DNP program. I thanked God for my second chance and was determined to finish the program. Three years later, tears filled my eyes when I was told by my committee chair that I successfully defended my scholarly project.

I was very thankful for the grace period. The ten years that I took to do the DNP degree was very rewarding. I was able to say that I was a student at Case Western Reserve University for ten years. The extra time afforded me the opportunity to have five committee members, including two different committee chairs. The requirement was to have a committee with three members, one being the chair. During the ten years that I was a student at Case Western, one chairperson and another committee member retired or resigned. Every member of my committee made a difference in my life and contributed to my scholarly project.

I also had to do the Collaborative Institutional Training Initiative (CITI) program three times. The CITI program was a requirement to do research using human subjects, and each certificate expired after one to three years depending on which part was done. Due to the length of time that I took to complete the DNP, two certificates expired, so I had to do that tedious course a third time. This program was done online and covered a lot of information. I had to do many of the quizzes more than once because after reading through the bulk of material, I did not remember most of what I read so I had to read it again. I was happy I persevered and completed this program because it was a requirement to do my scholarly project.

I also applied to the Institutional Review Board at Case Western Reserve University. The application process was challenging, but after several attempts and with the help of my committee chair, I completed and submitted the IRB application online. Thinking that this would be a long process, I resigned myself to waiting and not to think about it. I checked the website in a few days and was happy to see that there was a response. I gladly made the corrections that I was asked to make and re-submitted the application. Within a few weeks, the Institution Review Board gave me an exemption, so I was excited to start my project.

As was mentioned before, the final revision of my proposal was to determine nurse-midwives' knowledge and use of aromatherapy for pain relief during labor in the US. Having gotten my IRB exemption, I applied and received approval from an organization that certifies nurse-midwives to select subjects from their organization. I am grateful to this institution for sending out the survey questions to the nurse-midwives and for the willingness of the nurse-midwives to participate in the research. Seventy-five nurse-midwives participated in the survey. The data was analyzed, and the results reported in my scholarly project. I marveled at how time had changed. I remembered when I did my first research project more than twenty years before, I had to go to the hospital with paper copies of the survey and asked mothers and nurse-midwives to complete them. IRB approval was not needed but I got permission from the obstetric department chairperson to do my project. My research topic then was, "Does the presence of fathers in the delivery room have any effect on mothers' perception of pain." This process was time-consuming, but after several weeks, I had collected all my data. I am thankful that I completed my research in the one academic semester, which was the allotted time for the research.

The survey for my final research project was done online. Data collection was easier because an online survey tool analyzed and reported the data. I had to learn to do pie charts and bars on the computer to enhance the reporting of the data. I have seen that education is on ongoing process and one is never too old to learn new information.

Chapter 27
Final Defense

My final defense was scheduled for Monday, April 10, 2017 at Frances Payne Bolton School of Nursing at Case Western Reserve University in Cleveland, Ohio. My daughter and I travelled to Ohio and after checking into our hotel, we went for a walk. I did not go to the same section of Cleveland as on my previous visits. We walked around the area but did not find the university. We walked back to the hotel and I was happy to learn that there was a shuttle bus that ran from the hotel to the university. Relieved that the travel arrangements were made for my visit to the university the following day, I concentrated on my Power Point presentation that I spent several hours working on for the defense of my research project. I thought everything was done at home in New York, but I made some changes as I went through the slides. I went to bed feeling satisfied with the Power Point presentation. As I showered with the lavender-scented soap, I thought of my project. One of the essential oils used for Aromatherapy is lavender. I was very pleased to see that the soap, lotion, and shampoo in the bathroom of the hotel were made of lavender. I dressed in a back suit with a purple blouse, and my daughter's dress also had purple. Our clothes were deliberately chosen because I was told that purple is a royal color and it should be worn on important occasions. My daughter and I hurried outside of the hotel and boarded the bus at exactly 9:30 a.m. I was happy to be dropped off at the Frances Payne Bolton School of Nursing on the campus of Case Western Reserve University. I was also relieved that I had more than an hour to set up for the presentation and to ensure that everything worked well. I thought that the defense was at 10 a.m., but it was scheduled for 11 a.m. I also had more time to review my presentation.

The room had an oval-shaped table with six chairs, a smart board, and a chalkboard. My daughter wrote the title of my research project and my name with beautiful penmanship on the chalkboard. She wrote:

Nurse-Midwives' Knowledge and Use of
Aromatherapy for Pain Relief
during Labor in the US
Researched and presented by:
Paulette Terrelonge MSN, RN

This was possible because of the extra time that we had. The chairperson of my committee visited the room several times and enquired about my well-being, which relieved some of the anxiety I was feeling. I was happy to have an input in the preparation of the room, as the gentleman who brought the telephone into the room sought my advice on the placement of the telephone. The committee chair and one other member entered the room a few minutes to 11 a.m. The third member of the committee joined the conference via telephone. My daughter sat quietly in a corner in the room. I started the presentation promptly at 11 a.m. The half an hour allotted for the defense went quickly by. I was relaxed and presented my research findings with confidence. The instructions that I received from a faculty member at Case Western Reserve University and my daughter helped me in making several graphs. I had not done that type of graph before, so I found them very difficult to make. I almost gave up on trying, but I was glad I didn't because the graphs enhanced the presentation. I did not have the privileged of learning about computers until I was an adult, so my knowledge of the computer was limited.

The committee members asked several questions and I answered them to the best of my ability. The questions and answers lasted for about half an hour and then my daughter and I were asked to leave the room. We waited in a waiting area, and after about forty minutes, my committee chair called us to come back into the room. As we approached the room the committee member who preceded my daughter and I turned on the light and my daughter and I entered the room. I wondered why the light was off, then my committee chair said, "You passed." I was very elated and I hugged and thanked everyone in the room. I also thanked my committee member who was on the telephone. I accepted the congratulatory messages from all and then I was handed a gift and was told that it was from the alumni association. Upon opening the white box that contained the gift, I saw the most beautiful rectangular-shaped piece of thick glass with the inscription, "Dr. Paulette E. Terrelonge." It was then that I realize that my title had changed. I also received a card addressed to "Dr. Terrelonge." After the excitement was over, I was left with my committee chair and my daughter. I was told that there were some changes to be made to the final research paper but we would reconvene after lunch. My committee chair took my daughter and I to lunch at a restaurant near the university campus, and after a delicious lunch we went back to the university. I was given the corrections, but, feeling overwhelmed, my daughter and I were given permission to leave the university for the day. We were not sure how to get back to the hotel, so the secretary called the hotel and requested that the shuttle bus come for us. After a short ride, we were back at our hotel. I texted some of my friends and sent some of the photographs that my daughter took of me holding the plaque that was given to me. I enjoyed reading the congratulatory messages that some of my friends sent to me. My daughter and I ate the delicious meal that we bought for our dinner and then I started the task of correcting my research paper.

Chapter 28
The Home Stretch

C orrecting, correcting, correcting. I corrected my
proposal several times to get it as perfect as possible. I was grateful for the preparation that I received
early in the DNP program, which alerted me to the fact
that many revisions of my proposal would be needed. I
corrected my proposal with joy knowing that each correction made it better than the previous revision. The
input of my committee chair and the two other committee members was valuable.

I had four days to make the suggested corrections. I
planned to finish all the corrections by the third day and
submit my final paper, but that was not accomplished.
During the defense, one of my committee members
found that one of the participants in the study did not
meet the subject inclusion criteria. I had to manually go
through all the questions and removed all the responses
that the participant made. I had to recalculate all the per-
centages and remake the graphs, which took much time
because, as stated before, they were not easy to do. Some
days, I did not leave my hotel room. My daughter, who
accompanied me to Cleveland, went in search of food,
which gave me the necessary fuel to work on my project.

It was easier to use two computers to make the corrections. I had taken my laptop computer with me and
I used the hotel's computer as the second computer.

One night I spent three hours making corrections on my project and was happy with my accomplishments. I retired to bed after midnight and woke about 4 a.m. the following morning to complete the corrections. To my horror, the three hours of work that I had done the previous night was not saved. I was very disappointed but couldn't spend much time figuring out what happened, I just had to make those corrections again.

I needed a second computer, but I didn't trust the computer at the hotel anymore. I decided to use the computer in the computer lab at Case Western Reserve University. My journey to the university took me through the university hospital where my daughter and I had breakfast in the cafeteria. As I entered the computer lab at the university, I remembered the times before when I used that computer lab. The last time was many years ago. I completed what I thought was the last correction and sent it via email to my committee chair.

As was mentioned before, I had modified my research topic three times. Each research topic was corrected multiple times. It was also my practice to use two computers to facilitate the corrections of the proposals. I read the corrections from one computer and typed the corrections into the other computer. Previously, I printed the proposal with corrections, which took a lot of paper and ink, and this process would be repeated every time my committee chair returned my proposal. There were always corrections.

The cool Cleveland breeze and mild sunshine felt good on my skin, and as I inhaled the crisp air, I breathed a sigh of relief. The short walk to the university cafeteria where my daughter and I had lunch was invigorating.

After a delicious lunch I went for a walk to give my committee chair enough time to correct my paper again. The walk took my daughter and I to a contemporary art museum. Entering the silver building was hard to resist, and so we went in and looked around on the ground floor. We didn't spend much time in the art museum since I had to go back to my committee chair's office to get feedback on my project.

You guessed it! There were more corrections. I went back to the computer lab and repeated the process of correcting my project using two computers. There were fewer corrections than before and I was comforted by the thought that the end was very near. I then had to go through the entire paper making sure all the references were in and done properly. I found a footnote that had no reference and since I did not have the journal article with me, I had to delete some sentences and re-write the paragraph. I also found and deleted a reference that was not used in the paper. The name of a frequently referenced author was inadvertently changed by the spell checker on the computer. I had to manually go through the paper and correct the author's name, which was used frequently. I then scanned through the forty-eight-page paper, which included five pages of references. I submitted what I thought was the final paper, bid my committee chair farewell, and then went for a walk on the Cleveland streets.

I couldn't help but noticing how clean the streets were, and the beautiful buildings reminded me of London. I thought how privileged I was to be in Cleveland and hoped that an opportunity would arise for me to live in Cleveland. Our sightseeing came to an end with the buying of food and purchasing of ice scream from an ice scream parlor nearby. After a short walk back to our hotel room, we settled down to enjoy our last dinner in Cleveland and treated ourselves with the delicious ice cream.

I turned on the television for the first time in Cleveland. My daughter had some schoolwork that she was doing, even though she was on spring break from school, so she had not turned on the television either. One of the reasons was that she did not want to disturb me and I was grateful for her consideration. I needed quietness especially when I was searching for the participant who did not meet the subject inclusion criteria.

I retired to bed after a long and tiring day and promptly went to sleep. I woke early the following morning with the project on my mind. I read through the paper and would you believe that I found some errors? I corrected the errors that I saw and made another table. My flight was not until that afternoon and the project was due on the same day. I made my final trip to the Frances Payne Bolton School of Nursing at Case Western Reserve University, submitted my final paper, and bade my committee chair goodbye. I also went to the main office of the school of nursing to make sure that all the requirements were met for graduation.

Relieved that all the requirements were met, my daughter and I walked back to the hotel and completed our packing. There was just enough time to make it to the airport on time for our flight. With the check-out process completed at the hotel, I was happy that the driver of a taxi was waiting in the lobby of the hotel for passengers. Sitting in the back seat of the taxi, I reflected on my five-day trip to Cleveland and thanked God for a successful trip. After about half an hour we were at the airport.

Chapter 29
The Aftermath

The trip to the airport was uneventful and we got there just on time for our flight. After doing the check-in process at the machine, we proceeded to security. The line was long and I wondered if my daughter and I would get through in time for the flight. I was puzzled as my hand luggage was detained for further inspection. To the best of my recollection, there was none of the unauthorized items listed in the airport in my bag. I had been very careful in packing because an item that was in my hand luggage was discarded at the airport in New York on my way to Ohio.

I watched the security officer as she opened my hand luggage and used an object shaped like a wand to probe inside my bag. As she picked up the white box that contained my gift from the alumni association, I gasped. "Please Lord," I whispered, "Don't let her take that away." I had put the gift in my hand luggage because I thought it would be safer there than in my suitcase. She opened the box and scanned the rectangular piece of glass with my name and title inscribed on it. Since she did not remove the glass from its bubble-wrap covering, she did not know what was inside the box, neither did she know the value of the object she had just scanned.

I was relieved when she placed the box back into my luggage and closed the zipper. She beckoned to me to take the bag, so I picked it up and hurried to the assigned gate for my flight to New York. Safely at the gate, I sat in a chair and once again thanked God for allowing me to accomplish this final task of defending my scholarly project at Case Western Reserve University. The gift from the alumni association was a surprise, but I also thanked the Lord that it was not taken away from me.

With a little less than half an hour before the scheduled departure time of the flight, I opened my laptop and logged onto the National Certification Corporation (NCC) website. The NCC is the certifying body for the inpatient obstetrics examination that I successfully took more than twenty years prior to the writing of this book. I maintained the inpatient obstetric certification every three years by doing forty-five continuing education (CE) credits. Even though I had not worked in obstetrics for the past six years, I maintained the certification. I attended conferences and earned the required number of CE credits when I worked in obstetrics. After I became a school nurse, I did the required CEs online, which was very time-consuming. I struggled with the idea of not maintaining the inpatient obstetric certification three years before but, remembering how difficult the examination was, I did not want it to lapse. There was still a glimmer of hope that I might go back to work in obstetrics, but the hope got dimmer with each passing year. Three years came only too quickly. The recertification was due again. I earned five CEs from doing the mandatory assessment on the NCC website, but I did not acquire any more CEs in three years. I did some modules online but did not achieve passing grades. I purchased many modules but did not get a chance to read some of them. I was not able to achieve the forty-five required CEs that were needed for recertification by the deadline of March 15, so I had to let my certification lapse. I was planning to apply for an extension, but I was too busy preparing for my final defense less than one month away. This was a painful experience because I had maintained the certification for more than twenty years. I enjoyed using the initials RNC after my name, but I have to be satisfied with the letters PHN. My job as a public health nurse afforded me the privilege of using the title of PHN.

I searched the NCC website while I was at the airport in Cleveland and hoped that I could apply for an extension for renewing the certification but found out that the deadline for extension had also passed. My thoughts were interrupted because the boarding process started, and since my seat number was in the group number that was called, I had to quickly put away my laptop and join the line to board the aircraft. With my seat belt fastened, I closed my eyes, and soon I was in New York.

Chapter 30
Graduation

I initially said that I was not going to my graduation. My mind was quickly changed after I was told that I successfully defended my scholarly project. I remembered hearing that 1 percent of nurses have doctorate degrees. I was happy to be a part of that 1 percent and therefore thought it necessary to meet with the other graduates who shared similar experiences. The hotel where I spent five days while I was in Cleveland for my defense was fully booked for the graduation weekend. I left Cleveland determined to return for graduation but had no idea where I was going to stay.

I returned to New York and continued my search for a hotel. I was elated when I found a hotel over the Internet and did not hesitate to pay the nonrefundable fee for two nights. I searched the internet and found some possible flights, but for some reason I did not book any. I think that I was waiting to find cheaper ones. As graduation drew nearer, several friends expressed their desire to attend my graduation. I started to explore different possibilities of getting to Cleveland for my graduation so that my friends could go with me. The pursuit of renting a van came to an end when I couldn't get a suitable van, so the decision was made to hire my friend's van. That was the best decision as I was able to have my daughter and eight friends accompany me to my graduation.

We boarded the van the eve of graduation and started on an adventurous trip from Brooklyn to Cleveland. Our journey took us through four states: New York, New Jersey, Pennsylvania, then Ohio. We made about two stops along the way and, with the help of the GPS, arrived safely at our hotel about ten hours later. I also commended the driver of the van because he drove all the way. We arrived after 2 a.m. and our aim was to go to our rooms and get some sleep while it was still dark. The check-in process took longer than was expected, but we were very grateful to be finally in our rooms. The first thing I did was to hang my graduation gown in the closet. I had carefully packed the gown, hood, and cap in a small suitcase. I made sure that I visualized the suitcase before we left New York. There was no room for forgetfulness that day.

My anxiety was relieved when I received the graduation regalia about one week before graduation. It was Mother's Day and the enjoyment of my day was enhanced when I opened the box and saw the graduation gown, hood, and cap. I had gone downstairs and saw a box with my name. I picked up the box, and, without opening it, I started to feel relief. I opened the box as fast as I could and saw the most beautiful graduation gown. The gown was blue with black enclosing the zipper in the front. The sleeves had three horizontal black strips. The hood was peach and blue and the hat was black and shaped like a hexagon. Having graduated twice before in the US, I noted that the tassel on the cap could not be moved. It was permanently fixed to the left side of the cap. The cap was also shaped differently. The other caps were shaped like squares. As mentioned before, this cap was shaped like a hexagon.

I recalled Mother's Day ten years prior when I started the DNP program. I was not as happy as I felt ten years later. The experience that I had on that day taught me that, "Good things do not always come easy." I was going to Case Western Reserve University to do my second course. I waited at the assigned gate at JFK Airport in New York and watched the time pass for the scheduled departure of the airplane. The flight was delayed for eight hours. I spent most of my Mother's Day at the airport, but now I can say that it was for a "good thing."

What a difference ten years made! Graduation was nowhere in sight when I waited at the airport all those years ago. The realization that I was in Cleveland, Ohio, for my graduation brought tears to my eyes. This was my last trip to the university and I had started missing it already. I had the pleasure of saying that I was a student at Case Western Reserve University for ten years and soon I was going to be an alumnus. With just a few hours before daybreak, I went to bed and was awakened by the sound of an alarm. I jumped out of bed, but, realizing that it was still early, I went back to bed but could not sleep.

Graduation day finally arrived. My friends from the other rooms gathered in the room that I shared with another friend, her daughter, and my daughter. We had occupied four rooms but three of the rooms had to be vacated by 11 a.m. I had paid for an extra night for my room which we only used for an hour and a half. We had breakfast, and then my friends assisted me in getting ready. I felt like a celebrity because of the amount of attention that was given to me. We finally checked out of the hotel and with the help of the GPS, we went to the reception for the graduation.

I was amazed to see the large number of nurses who were graduating. I learned later that there were fifty-six DNP graduates. The fruits, vegetables, and other foods that were provided were welcome because our next meal would be at least ten hours after graduation. We did not stop on the road to get food as our aim was to get home as soon as possible. There were three students who had to go to school the following morning and some of the adults had to go to work. The short procession from the reception ended and soon we were entering the church, which was the venue for the graduation. As I walk down the aisle, I looked around for my daughter and my friends who were all standing as the graduates marched in. The church was packed with people who had gathered to witness the graduation of their loved ones. I did not see my friends at the beginning of the graduation ceremony, but I later saw my daughter and one of my friends taking photographs of me.

After being ushered to my seat, I quickly flipped through the pages of the program and found my name listed under the graduates. I thanked God for this accomplishment and was reminded of a passage in the Bible that said that when God allowed us to do something, He will see us through to its completion. Ten long years of writing papers and of trying to get time off from work to attend classes in various places had come to an end. Some of the places where I attended classes were Connecticut, Ohio, and St. Kitts. I hurried to receive my degree when my name was called, and I was hooded by my committee chair. My daughter seized every moment she could to take photographs of me. It so happened that I was sitting at the end of a row and near to a door, so picture-taking was made easier. I was congratulated by my committee, my friends, my daughter, and well-wishers.

The graduation ceremony lasted over an hour, for which I was very thankful. It gave us enough time to meet my committee and other faculty members and to take photographs. I looked for other familiar faces, but I did not find any. I concluded that all the students whom I'd met before must have graduated already. After all, the seven allotted years for the DNP program were gone. I tried hard to forget the past and to concentrate on the present. I took a lot of photographs with my friends and could have easily spent more time meeting and greeting others, but the ten-hour drive to New York was in my thoughts. We boarded the van that brought us to Ohio and headed to the university bookstore to return the graduation gown and hood. My temporary ownership of the graduation gown and hood was short-lived, but I was allowed to keep the cap, which made me happy. The small suitcase that carried my graduation apparel went back to New York empty.

The ten-hour journey back to New York City was full of excitement. We sang many songs, which lasted for hours. Some of the songs brought back memories as I had not sung them since I was a child. Once in New York, we dropped off a few of my friends at their homes, some of us left in our cars parked on the street near our church where we'd left them, and the driver and another friend continued their journey to Queens. We thanked God for taking us all home and for the driver who did all the driving.

Chapter 31
A Heart of Gratitude

O ne of the most frequently asked questions was what I was going to do now that I had a doctorate degree. My answer was that I was going to continue to do what I was doing before. I was a school nurse when I completed the doctorate degree. I told someone that the children who attended the school where I worked needed my service and that I was not going to leave because I had a doctorate degree. I was very grateful to earn a doctorate degree and I wanted to give back to my community. I worked in the same school district where I lived and where my daughter attended three public schools.

My profound thanks to the Lord of the universe who made everything possible. God knew me from before I was formed in my mother's womb, as stated by Jeremiah in the Bible. God orchestrated my life and implanted the thought of being a nurse from the time I was seven years old. He kept me all of my life and allowed me to study nursing and midwifery and pursue a nurse practitioner's degree and finally a doctorate degree in nursing.

Special thanks to my committee who worked tirelessly to ensure that I met all the requirements for graduation. I also want to thank the five nurse-midwives who reviewed the questionnaire and gave me feedback, the institution and the nurse-midwives who participated in the study, the nurses' union and the institution that paid most of the tuition, and everyone at Case Western Reserve University who had anything to do with me being at the university and for helping in any way. I also want to thank all the schools, colleges, and universities that I attended.

I want to say a special thanks to my dear friend who planned and executed a party for me. The party was meant to be a surprise, but some of my friends called me to say that they couldn't attend. I laughed and told them that I was not the one to call, but I was grateful to know that they called. I also want to say thanks to another friend who made sure that I was presentable for the party. She did my hair, and I know that if she had more time, I might have been totally transformed.

My church family also had a great part to play. They came to the party, gave gifts and tributes, helped in cooking, worked in the kitchen, decorated the hall, picked up supplies, planned the program, sang, and much more. My two friends who were most instrumental in my party were also members of my church. I also want to thank the administration of my church for granting the approval for the party to be held at the church.

I also want to thank my children who also played active roles. My son escorted me to my seat at the head table and my daughter helped to decorate the hall, serve meals to the head table, was the photographer, and helped me to select my dress. Both of my children gave beautiful tributes. My grandchildren and daughter-in-law also played significant roles. They sat at the head table and I was happy that I had a family. How can I say thanks to my sister-in-law and friend who travelled from Florida to New York to celebrate this special moment with me?

There were other visitors who were not members of my church, but they also played significant roles. Some of the members of Globally Commissioned Evangelists were also in attendance. Globally Commissioned Evangelists is a prayer/evangelistic ministry of which I am a member. There were friends from New York, New Jersey, and Pennsylvania. Special thanks to the master of ceremonies who came all the way from New Jersey and did an excellent job.

I also want to thank a sister from another church who came and sang although she did not know me very well. One of the attendees of the party was a nurse who migrated to the US with me almost thirty years before. We also worked together at the same hospital for about three and a half years before I went on a leave of absence to Jamaica. We've kept in touch all these years. She supported me when my mother died and visited me in the hospital during my last hospitalization.

I am in no way saying that I have arrived, but I am open and waiting on my next assignment from the Lord. The souvenir cups that were given to the guests at my party had words that were penned by Jerimiah. The words were, "I know the plans that you have for me." Two of the signees on the beautiful card that I received wrote these words: "Higher than the highest human thoughts is God's ideal for his Children."

Being a nurse is a blessing. I am thankful for the educational opportunities that existed that allowed me to pursue higher degrees. My nursing union reimbursed all my tuition cost for my bachelor's and master's degrees, for which I am thankful. I paid only about 10 percent of the cost of tuition for my doctorate degree. Thanks to the hospital that invested in the education of the advanced practice nurses.

I met some very helpful people along the way as I climbed my mountains. They assisted me as I reached for the stars and followed my dreams. Their encouraging words propelled me along, and I am happy that I am in this noble profession called nursing.

CPSIA information can be obtained
at www.ICGtesting.com
Printed in the USA
FFHW022145301018
49120794-53352FF

9 781545 622643